W9-ATN-501

**SPIRITED RECIPES FROM
ASHEVILLE'S NEW SOUTH KITCHEN**

TUPELO HONEY CAFE

Spirited Recipes from
Asheville's New South Kitchen

Elizabeth Sims with Chef Brian Sonoskus

Foreword by Kim Sunee

Photography by Brie Williams

**Andrews McMeel
Publishing, LLC**
Kansas City • Sydney • London

TUPELO HONEY CAFE

Text copyright © 2011 Tupelo Honey Cafe. Photography copyright © 2011 Brie Williams. All rights reserved. Printed in China. No part of this book may be used or reproduced in any manner whatsoever without written permission except in the case of reprints in the context of reviews. For information, write Andrews McMeel Publishing, LLC, an Andrews McMeel Universal company, 1130 Walnut Street, Kansas City, Missouri 64106.

11 12 13 14 15 SDB 10 9 8 7 6 5 4 3 2 1

ISBN: 978-1-4494-0064-4

Library of Congress Control Number: 2010930542

Photography: Brie Williams
Design: Julie Barnes
Food Stylist: Kim Sunee
Prop Stylist: Martha Dugger
Book Layout: Diane Marsh

Page 2, reprinted with permission of the author from *A Gracious Plenty: Recipes and Recollections from the American South* by John T. Edge. Copyright © 1999 by Ellen Rolfes Books, Inc., and the Center for the Study of Southern Culture, University of Mississippi. Published by G.P. Putnam's Sons.

Page 50, reprinted with the permission of Scribner, a Division of Simon & Schuster, Inc., from *Look Homeward, Angel* by Thomas Wolfe. Copyright © 1929 by Charles Scribner's Sons. Copyright renewed © 1957 by Edward C. Ashwell, Administrator, C.T.C. and/or Fred W. Wolfe. All rights reserved.

Page 77, reprinted with permission of the author from *Long Time Leaving: Dispatches from Up South* by Roy Blount, Jr. Copyright © 2006 by Roy Blount, Jr. Published by Alfred A. Knopf, Inc.

Page 99, reprinted with permission of the author from *One Fell Soup: Or I'm Just a Bug on the Windshield of Life* by Roy Blount, Jr. Copyright © 1982 by Roy Blount, Jr. Published by Penguin.

Pages 133, 145, from *Bill Neal's Southern Cooking: Revised and Enlarged Edition* by Bill Neal. Copyright © 1989 by William Franklin Neal. Used with permission of the publisher. www.uncpress.unc.edu

Page 166, reprinted with permission of the author from *Southern Food: At Home, on the Road, in History* by John Egerton. Copyright © 1989 by John Egerton. Published by Alfred A. Knopf, Inc.

Page 204, reprinted with permission of the author from *A Love Affair with Southern Cooking: Recipes and Recollections* by Jean Anderson. Copyright © 2007 by Jean Anderson. Published by William Morrow Cookbooks.

Photographs used with permission from The Biltmore Company, Asheville, North Carolina: p. 106–107; North Carolina Collection, Pack Memorial Library, Asheville, North Carolina: p. xiii, xv, 41, 80, 91, 102, 161, 167, 200; Thomas Wolfe Collection, Pack Memorial Library, Asheville, North Carolina: p. 50.

www.andrewsmcmeel.com
www.tupelohoneycafe.com

ATTENTION: SCHOOLS AND BUSINESSES
Andrews McMeel books are available at quantity discounts with bulk purchase for educational, business, or sales promotional use. For information, please write to: Special Sales Department, Andrews McMeel Publishing, LLC, 1130 Walnut Street, Kansas City, Missouri 64106.

I dedicate this book to my children, Rachel and Walter. They have proved time after time the power of love and grace and the strength that comes from believing in yourself. May their tables always be filled with laughter and joy.

CONTENTS

ACKNOWLEDGMENTS viii

FOREWORD xi

INTRODUCTION: From the Heart of Asheville, Tupelo Honey's Eclectic Table xiii

CHAPTER 1   The Larder 1

CHAPTER 2   Angels of the First Degree: Heavenly Appetizers and Soups 43

CHAPTER 3   The Art of the Perfect Sandwich and Salad 69

CHAPTER 4   Fish Out of Water 97

CHAPTER 5   Chicken Seven Ways, or We Still Lay 123

CHAPTER 6   Beyond the Smokehouse 143

CHAPTER 7   The Threes 165

CHAPTER 8   Blue Ridge Parkway Brunches 185

CHAPTER 9   As Sweet as Tupelo Honey 203

RESOURCES 216

METRIC CONVERSIONS AND EQUIVALENTS 216

INDEX 218

ACKNOWLEDGMENTS

I am extremely grateful to everyone at Tupelo Honey Cafe for allowing me to be part of the family. I owe particular thanks to owner Steve Frabitore, who took a chance on me, and Chef Brian Sonoskus, whose amazing recipes fill this book. I'd also like to thank our partners at Andrews McMeel, especially our editor, Jean Lucas, our terrific art director, Julie Barnes, and AM president Kirsty Melville. I appreciate their collective leap of faith, and their embracement of our city and Tupelo Honey Cafe with enthusiastic support.

Lots of hard work went into this book, and it wouldn't be here without the creative and culinary brilliance of Kim Sunee, the beautiful photography by Brie Williams, and the keen eye and detective skills of Martha Dugger.

I am also deeply indebted to all of my friends and colleagues at the Southern Foodways Alliance, an organization that I hold dear. SFA is a group of thinkers, cooks, chefs, historians, foodies, journalists, authors, and academicians who take a long look at the South and see a region with a variety of food reflecting the diversity of people, places, traditions, and histories. Mainly, SFA is like my family, and I am honored to be a part of it. I am especially grateful to my friends Ronni Lundy, John Egerton, and John T. Edge for their guidance and insight.

Finally, I am grateful to my siblings Mary Jane, Roger, and Luz who have kept the memories of our mom's table and our grandmothers' tables alive and well. I honor my grandmothers, Mary Emma Murrey Lusby, who made the best warm fried pies and caramel cake in the universe, and Myrtle McClure Brown, whose reverence for the abundance of the Appalachian region I now share. And most important, I am deeply grateful to my mother, Miriam Lusby Brown, who nourished me in so many ways every day.

—Elizabeth Sims

I would like to thank the following people for the roles they have played in my life. First, my family for the origins of comfort food. Jack Baker's Lobster Shanty for teaching me to be an awesome line cook. Sharon Schott Prosser and Stephen D. Frabitore for their vision. Martha Palmer for pickled beets and garlic ranch dressing, Micah Harwell for salsa verde, Daniel Wright for candied almonds, and Jamie White for pickled green tomato salad and fresh mozzarella and cherry apple chowchow. Fran Scibelli for her uncompromising values and taste. The people of Asheville for their support and mostly Kate and Jack for their patience and understanding. Thank you food world for the best career possible and thanks to the cookbook team.

—Brian Sonoskus

As the owner of Tupelo Honey Cafe, I've listened to customers from all across the country say they couldn't wait to eat with us. I've watched longtime staff continue to deliver incredible service and amazing food, day after day, with the same enthusiasm that began when the restaurant opened in 2000. I had to make this happen. I knew people wanted this book. And more important, I knew that the restaurant and all the folks who make the restaurant really deserve this book. I was fortunate to find the right partners in Andrews McMeel and am extremely proud of what our team has produced. I hope that you will enjoy these great recipes at home and that you will come see us if your travels ever lead you to Asheville.

—Steve Frabitore

FOREWORD

BY KIM SUNEE

Southerners have deep food memories, and one of my favorite memories growing up in New Orleans is that of being at my grandfather's table. Aside from our raucous family of twelve, there were a few lonesome stragglers my grandfather would often invite to join us. Once we had our first spoonfuls of steaming crawfish bisque, Sunday pot roast, or seafood gumbo, silence united us all. We suddenly understood that we were loved; we knew someone had taken great care to nourish us.

I remembered this feeling when I savored my first bites at Tupelo Honey Cafe. Here, I thought, is a place with food that makes you feel good, that you want to share with loved ones. Here is a table that will always welcome you back—with sugar and bacon, pecans and cream, grits and dredge, pimento and greens. I've traveled all around the world and dined at many fine tables in cities such as Paris, Florence, New York, and Hong Kong. The best tables for me always convey what I found at Tupelo Honey Cafe in Asheville: No matter where you started out or how far you may roam, a meal here means that you're home.

Tupelo Honey Cafe represents what is best about Asheville, a city that celebrates a unique generosity of spirit and an eclectic gathering of people, visible in its artist communities and at the table. Unlike other places in the South, the city and Tupelo Honey Cafe pride themselves on "coloring outside the lines." Chef Brian Sonoskus and his crew demonstrate this in the kitchen with a love of bold flavors while maintaining respect for tradition. Offering the best from local farmers and the bounty of the Blue Ridge Mountains, Brian cooks up everything from classic greens and toasted sesame seed coleslaw to fried green tomatoes over cheese grits, Southern fried chicken BLT, and sweet potato pancakes. All food that comforts.

I'm excited that this book now offers the chance to cook these deeply satisfying recipes at home. If you can't get to Tupelo Honey Cafe, this book will give you the flavor of the city of Asheville and some of the best things you'll ever put in your mouth.

INTRODUCTION: FROM THE HEART OF ASHEVILLE, TUPELO HONEY'S ECLECTIC TABLE

Not only is it okay to color outside the lines here. It's expected.

Asheville is a city that takes *unique* to a new level. And, like the sweet golden elixir for which we are named, Tupelo Honey Cafe is a rarity as well. That's why we like to think about experiencing our food as an important part of experiencing our city.

We are located in North Carolina, but we are not Southern like Charleston or Savannah or Birmingham or Nashville. Neither are we strictly soup beans and corn bread Appalachian although we are certainly proud of our mountain heritage. We aren't entirely bohemian, but we definitely embrace that spirit. Nor are we simply an easygoing place to vacation or spend your golden years, although we welcome that identity as well. Whatever your view of us, when you visit, you will witness how we love to celebrate our independent streak.

We are home to artists and musicians, religious conference centers, New Age enthusiasts, writers, yoga practitioners, multimedia innovators, healers of every stripe, and technology groundbreakers. We welcome road cyclists, hikers, rock climbers, mountain bikers, llama trekkers, kayakers, and backpackers. We rejoice in quiet meditation and contemplation and the sound of a porch swing on a summer's night. Or the beat of the drum circle on Friday evenings or the bluegrass that reverberates across town, undulating with the wind.

Downtown Asheville c. 1887

We are an eclectic town, full of colorful and diverse individuals, creative energy, and engaging ideas. With an acceptance not always found in small cities, people who live and work and play here—as well as people who visit here—all feel at home.

At Tupelo Honey Cafe, we like to think all of these ingredients that make our town so special come together around our collective table. And that we nourish exchanges through dialogue and debate, togetherness and tradition, and family

and friends, both old and new. The recipes in this book reflect the rich fabric of the restaurant and the joy with which we cook—Pan-Fried Pork Chops with Black-Eyed Pea and Andouille Sausage Ragout, Sweet Potato Pancakes with Peach Butter and Spiced Pecans, Chicken Apple Meat Loaf with Tarragon Tomato Gravy, Shrimp and Goat Cheese Grits with Roasted Red Pepper Sauce. It's food meant for savoring, sharing, remembering.

Since its early days as a drovers' town, Asheville has been a crossroad for trading—commerce, of course, but perhaps more important, ideas. With the advent of the railroad in the late 1800s, the town soon gained a reputation as a resort community and an escape from the summer heat of the Carolina Low Country. Western North Carolina also became a resort playground for the elite from the Northeast, many of them coming for the mountain air and to "take the waters" at area hot springs. As a result, many people from different regions of the country have left their mark on our community.

Some of them have been home boys, like Thomas Wolfe and George Pack. Some have

come from elsewhere—George Vanderbilt, for example, or F. Scott Fitzgerald or Bob Moog or Buckminster Fuller. Each has added something to our mountain stew—our Blue Ridge burgoo—making it richer and more dynamically palatable with each spoonful.

So we think it makes sense that our food at Tupelo Honey Cafe reflects the diversity of people and ideas that seem to thrive in Asheville. We embrace the idea of our town being a food lover's Foodtopia—an idealistic destination committed to delivering to people who care about food and drink—with all of its amazing restaurants, tailgate markets, and microbreweries. We are proud to serve you the food we get from our terrific farmer partners and from Sunshot Organics, our own farm (where we grow some of our vegetables and berries and even the flowers for our garnishes). We believe in our citywide commitment to Foodtopian truth, understanding our obligation to deliver a taste of our city and our mountains with honesty and integrity.

Our restaurant is a busy place in the middle of our busy and bustling downtown. Our staff, with the artistic flair of a dance troupe, orches-

trates and choreographs their ins and outs from the open kitchen to your table. They add to the energy of Tupelo, something you feel the minute you walk in. It's akin to Asheville's steady, strong, soulful heartbeat.

As a Foodtopian society, we were excited when an online poll conducted by Charlie Papazian—beer sage and home brew book author—named Asheville Beer City USA in 2009 and 2010, but is it any wonder? With ten microbreweries and the blossoming agricultural trend toward growing hops and barley in our mountains, Asheville may also be considered a Brewtopia. At Tupelo Honey Cafe, we love working with our local brewmasters—including The French Broad Brewing Company, Pisgah Brewing, Green Man, and Highland Brewing—to constantly create new and seasonal profiles for our local-only taps. And our staff is incredibly knowledgeable about which beers pair best with whatever you order, from Fried Green Tomatoes with Goat Cheese Basil Grits to your favorite cut of local beef with Tomato Shallot Gravy.

If you haven't been to Asheville or to Tupelo, we hope you'll see this book as an invitation to come experience what we have to offer. If you do visit, we hope your experience at Tupelo Honey Cafe is as memorable as your Asheville experience, whether you call our mountains home or are visiting our community from somewhere else. Real tupelo honey comes from bees that thrive on rare tupelo trees, so you won't find it just anyplace. Its distinctive floral flavor changes with each year, depending on the environment and how prolific the trees—and bees—are. We believe our town and our restaurant are pretty special, too: a uniquely sweet spot to stop and break bread.

So, take these recipes home and share a little slice of Tupelo Honey Cafe with your family and friends. Envision driving on the Blue Ridge Parkway, absorbing the glorious mountain vistas. Imagine a weekend filled with the sensual, from heartfelt bluegrass or indie rock to an art gallery stroll along the riverfront. Celebrate the spirit of independence. Spread a big table or a small one, but be sure you plan for some lively discussion and discourse.

Just remember, at Tupelo Honey Cafe, you are always welcome to come back for seconds.

NOTES ON WINE AND BEER PAIRINGS

In keeping with Tupelo Honey Cafe's approach to food, our beer and wine pairings are intended to wake up your taste buds, complementing the dish and bringing its best flavors forward. We also believe the best beer or wine pairing is up to the individual—there is no right or wrong choice, in other words.

It may be a new idea to you to pair food with beers and styles of beer. Asheville has over ten microbreweries feverishly brewing some of the best beer in America. So, we're a little spoiled. But at the restaurant, we encourage folks to try one of our beer flights with their food, testing one style of brew with this food, another style with that food. It's fun, of course, but it also illustrates how many foods just pair better with beer.

You will see beer and wine suggestions throughout the cookbook, with beers denoted by a mug icon and wines denoted by a wineglass icon. These are simply suggestions, and we have left them purposefully broad and with lots of room for you to be the judge in choosing which Cabernet Sauvignon you like or which Irish stout suits your fancy.

So, clink! Here's to you.

BREWS NEWS
Asheville's numerous breweries and brewpubs lend a relaxed vibe to the dining scene and the city's nightlife. The city comes alive with beer aficionados during its annual Brewgrass Festival each September, a nationally recognized gathering of microbreweries and renowned bluegrass musicians. The community even has its own guided brewery tour—Asheville Brews Cruise—allowing imbibers of craft beers to taste and tour across the city with both van and walking behind-the-scene experiences.

THE LARDER

SALSAS

Apple Salsa

Peach Fennel Salsa

Roasted Corn Salsa

Green Tomato Salsa

Sunshot Salsa

GRAVIES AND SAUCES

Milk Gravy

Sausage Gravy

Creamy Red-Eye Gravy

Cremini Sweet Onion Gravy

Tomato Shallot Gravy

Low Country Gravy

Cherry Truffle Sauce

Orange Cilantro Sauce

Smoked Tomato Sauce

Basic Barbecue Sauce

Tupelo Honey Wing Sauce

Smoked Jalapeño Sauce

Coffee Molasses Barbecue Sauce

Root Beer–Sorghum
Molasses Glaze

DRESSINGS AND SPREADS

Basil Vinaigrette

Spicy Smoked
Tomato Vinaigrette

Garlic Ranch Dressing

Pecan Vinaigrette

Creamy Maple
Mustard Dressing

Basil Cashew Pesto

Raspberry Honey Mayonnaise

Cranberry Mayonnaise

Smoked Jalapeño Aioli

PRESERVES AND PICKLES

Blueberry Preserves

Blackberry Skillet Jam

Cherry Apple Chowchow

Peach Butter

Pickled Sweet Onions

"There's a Memphis Minnie song called 'Selling My Pork Chops.' The refrain is 'I'm selling my pork chops, but I'm giving my gravy away.' Gravy is a personal expression of the soul. You can't sell gravy."

—Roy Blount Jr., from
A Gracious Plenty by John T. Edge

The larder was originally the smokehouse where bacon was stored, but these days, its meaning is more closely associated with the general kitchen pantry. The original larder was a pretty sacred spot, housing the salty sustenance of most Appalachian farms. And we think the pantry should still house the soul of the cook. It's where all good cooks go for inspiration and to grab their most go-to ingredients—spices and herbs, oils, baking essentials, cooking wines, vinegars and sauces, mustards, nuts, pickles, and preserves.

At Tupelo Honey, our pantry is full of magic. The magic is all about our commitment to the integrity of our kitchen and our belief in honoring and respecting our food, the farmers who grow it, the culinary creativity that inspires it, the hands that prepare it and serve it, and the appreciative friends who love it. We are proud to open our larder to you. Just remember, it's all about the fun of experimenting and discovering the personal combinations of tastes and tones that make your mouth sing.

Salsas

You could argue that salsas in all configurations of ingredients and taste profiles are the new ketchup on tables around the South. In truth, these delicious complements to a meal are a close cousin to the well-established tradition of canning and pickling fresh produce for the pantry. Salsas are more of a carpe diem way of savoring the garden at its height.

Our salsas reflect the bounty of southern Appalachia, and certainly using fresh ingredients from the farm is ideal. But today's groceries and markets offer many produce items year-round, so it is possible to make a fresh salsa, even in December. In fact, our Peach Fennel Salsa can use canned peaches, and the green apples in our Apple Salsa are easily available all year. We're a little biased, however, when it comes to our Sunshot Salsa. You just have to have the freshest ingredients possible to really ace this one, so enjoy it before the last days of summer are gone.

In western North Carolina, fall means apple harvest, and we love playing with the many different local varieties, including heirloom apples, grown here. We prefer the tartness of a granny smith contrasted with the heat of the peppers to make this salsa. It's perfect with a savory pork dish like our Root Beer Molasses–Glazed Pork Tenderloin with Smoked Jalapeño Sauce and Apple Salsa (page 149). You may want to add a tablespoon of lime juice for a more liquid consistency.

APPLE SALSA

2 Granny Smith apples, diced

1 medium poblano pepper, seeded and diced

1 large red bell pepper, seeded and diced

½ large sweet onion (such as Vidalia), diced

2 tablespoons tupelo honey

⅛ teaspoon sea salt

⅛ teaspoon freshly ground black pepper

1 tablespoon minced fresh parsley

Combine the apples, poblano pepper, bell pepper, and onion in a large bowl and add the honey, salt, pepper, and parsley. Serve immediately or refrigerate in an airtight container for up to 2 days.

MAKES 3 CUPS

Peaches are in abundance at our farmer's markets during the height of summer. It's no coincidence, then, that this salsa goes so well with a summer grill-out, especially grilled chicken salad. The fennel adds a note of anise as a counterpoint to the lushness of the fruit. While fresh peaches are best, you can also use canned peaches. Be sure you drain them of all syrup. Try this delicious side with our Char-Grilled Pork Tenderloin with Peach Fennel Salsa (page 155).

PEACH FENNEL SALSA

½ cup diced fresh fennel (bulb, stalk, and feathery leaves, tough outer layer discarded)

2 cups peeled and diced peaches (about 4 large peaches)

1 cup diced roasted red bell pepper

½ cup diced red onion

4 teaspoons roasted garlic oil (see box)

⅛ teaspoon sea salt

⅛ teaspoon freshly ground black pepper

Combine the fennel, peaches, bell peppers, onion, garlic oil, salt, and pepper in a large bowl. Refrigerate in an airtight container for at least 30 minutes. The salsa can be kept refrigerated for 2 days.

MAKES 2½ CUPS

ROASTED GARLIC PUREE AND ROASTED GARLIC OIL
Another basic in our pantry, roasted garlic puree is the end product of simmering 12 to 14 garlic cloves over medium heat in 1 cup olive oil in a saucepan for about 20 minutes, or until the garlic turns golden brown. Strain the oil, reserving the garlic, and use the oil for sautés, salad dressings, and marinades. Puree the garlic cloves in a food processor until it forms a smooth paste. Refrigerate for up to 2 weeks.

When fresh corn is up in our mountains, we love to use bicolored varieties to make this summer salsa as colorful as it is delicious. It's a versatile accompaniment but particularly good with seared fish or garden vegetable quesadillas. Try our Bronzed Wild Sockeye Salmon with Roasted Corn Salsa (page 120).

ROASTED CORN SALSA

2 cups fresh corn, cut from 3 or 4 large cobs

1 tablespoon extra-virgin olive oil

¼ teaspoon sea salt

⅛ teaspoon freshly ground black pepper

1 cup diced red bell pepper (about 1 large pepper)

1 cup diced green bell pepper (about 1 large pepper)

1 cup diced red onion (about 2 small onions)

¼ cup seeded and diced mild banana pepper

1 tablespoon minced fresh sage

Dash of cayenne pepper

Stir the corn and olive oil together on a rimmed sheet pan and roast at 400°F for about 7 minutes, or until it is a golden, caramelized color. Let cool slightly. Combine the roasted corn, salt, black pepper, red bell pepper, green bell pepper, onion, banana pepper, sage, and cayenne in a large bowl. Refrigerate the salsa in an airtight container for 3 to 5 days.

MAKES 2½ CUPS

Chef Brian Sonoskus

Who says green tomatoes are best fried? While we do like them that way, here's another take on the crisp, tart zing of a Southern-style salsa. It's mildly spicy and won't overwhelm your taste buds. It's featured in our Mushroom Quesadilla with Green Tomato Salsa and Smoked Jalapeño Sauce (page 56).

GREEN TOMATO SALSA

2 cups diced green tomatoes
(about 4 medium green
tomatoes)

½ cup diced red bell pepper

½ cup diced roasted red bell
pepper

Juice of 1 lime

1 large jalapeño, seeded, cored,
and minced

2 tablespoons minced fresh
cilantro

¼ teaspoon sea salt

¼ teaspoon freshly ground
black pepper

Combine all the ingredients and refrigerate in an airtight container for at least 30 minutes. This salsa can be kept refrigerated for 3 to 5 days.

MAKES 2½ CUPS

This salsa is named for our farm north of Asheville and capitalizes on the plentiful crop of cucumbers and tomatoes harvested across the region in the summertime. We love to use heirloom tomatoes like Cherokee Purple and Brandywine. It's the ideal refreshing sidekick to grilled salmon or with our Blackened Catfish with Sunshot Salsa (page 109).

SUNSHOT SALSA

1 cup diced tomato (about 1 large tomato)

1 cup peeled, seeded, and diced cucumber (about 1 large cucumber)

1 large red bell pepper, diced

1 large yellow bell pepper, diced

½ cup diced red onion

1 small jalapeño pepper, seeded and minced

Juice of ½ lime

2 teaspoons minced fresh cilantro

½ to 1 teaspoon green hot pepper sauce, depending on your love of spiciness

½ teaspoon sea salt

½ teaspoon freshly ground black pepper

Combine all the ingredients in a large bowl. Cover and let rest for 1 hour to allow the flavors to combine. This salsa can be refrigerated in an airtight container for 3 to 5 days.

MAKES 3 CUPS

Gravies and Sauces

We love good hot biscuits at Tupelo Honey Cafe and so do our patrons. In fact, we get more mail about our biscuits than just about anything else. So, our love of the unadulterated biscuit is pretty fierce and the idea of topping it with anything besides some butter and homemade preserves, a drizzle of honey, or a slab of salty country ham always gives us pause. Consequently, our dedication to gravy is serious. And we love it creamy, tangy, savory, earthy, spicy, soothing, jazzy—and frequently, atop a flaky biscuit.

We also love our local sorghum and incorporate it into our Coffee Molasses Barbecue Sauce and our Root Beer–Sorgham Molasses Glaze. One of our other staples at Tupelo is our Smoked Jalapeño Sauce, which is often the primary DNA for many recipes you'll find throughout the book, such as our Chicken Andouille Stir-Fry with Orange Jalapeño Glaze (page 134) and our Root Beer Molasses–Glazed Pork Tenderloin with Smoked Jalapeño Sauce and Apple Salsa (page 149).

A deliciously creamy and simple-to-make gravy for your biscuits. It's a great vegetarian option with its flavorful richness, but it really shines when paired with a plate of crisp, nutty-tasting fried chicken.

MILK GRAVY

2 tablespoons unsalted butter

¼ cup all-purpose flour

2 cups whole milk

¾ teaspoon sea salt, or as needed

½ teaspoon freshly ground black pepper

⅛ teaspoon cayenne pepper

In a heavy saucepan, melt the butter over low heat. Add the flour and whisk to combine. Increase the heat to medium and stir the mixture constantly for 2 minutes. You want to be sure the mixture does not brown. Slowly whisk in the milk and add the salt. Cook over medium heat, stirring constantly with a wooden spoon for about 5 minutes, or until the mixture thickens and coats the spoon. Add the black pepper and cayenne. Taste and add more salt, if needed. Remove from the heat and serve, or cool and refrigerate in an airtight container for up to 1 week.

MAKES 2 CUPS

We have wonderful locally made sausage in our neck of the woods, and this rich and filling gravy on biscuits does us proud every time. A side of eggs and you've got a breakfast that will keep you going. At least until lunch.

SAUSAGE GRAVY

4 ounces ground pork

1½ teaspoons unsalted butter

2 tablespoons plus 1½ teaspoons all-purpose flour

3 cups half-and-half

1 to 2 teaspoons sea salt

Freshly ground black pepper

In a frying pan, crumble and brown the pork on high heat until no longer pink. Reduce the heat to medium, add the butter, and stir until melted. Add the flour and cook 4 to 5 minutes, stirring constantly, until slightly browned. Continue stirring while adding the half-and-half and 1 teaspoon of the salt. Return the heat to high and whisk constantly for about 5 minutes, or until thickened. Add the pepper and more salt to taste and serve immediately, or store in an airtight container for up to 7 days.

MAKES APPROXIMATELY 3 CUPS

Red-eye gravy is a Southern tradition and, like many Southern traditions, was probably born out of necessity and a little invention. After cooking bacon or country ham in a cast-iron skillet, some ingenious cook decided to pour some leftover cold coffee in the pan and maximize its porcine residuals. We like ours with a little cream, just to be different. This gravy is great on eggs, grits, and biscuits, of course, but try it on meat loaf as well.

CREAMY RED-EYE GRAVY

¼ cup diced baked Virginia ham

¼ cup diced country ham

2 strips bacon, diced

½ cup diced Vidalia onion

1 tablespoon all-purpose flour

1 cup chicken stock

½ cup brewed coffee

½ cup heavy cream

¼ teaspoon freshly ground black pepper

In a heavy saucepan, combine the baked ham, country ham, bacon, and onion on high heat for 5 to 7 minutes, stirring until the bacon is browned and the onion is translucent. Stir in the flour and stir for 3 to 5 minutes, making a roux (page 17). Add the stock and coffee and bring to a boil. Reduce the heat to medium and simmer for 2 minutes. Add the cream, return the heat to high, and bring to a boil for 2 minutes, stirring constantly. Turn off the heat and stir in the pepper. Serve immediately, or cool and refrigerate in an airtight container for up to 1 week.

MAKES 2 CUPS

This recipe specifically calls for cremini mushrooms and Vidalia onions. The earthiness of the cremini hits the bass notes of this gravy while the sweetness of Vidalia plays the fiddle. You can make it with other types of mushrooms and onions, but it won't measure up to this version. It's to die for on a country-fried steak.

CREMINI SWEET ONION GRAVY

1½ cups cremini mushrooms, sliced thick (about 4 ounces)

1 large Vidalia onion, thinly sliced

2 tablespoons olive oil

2 cups demi-glace (see box)

½ teaspoon sea salt

½ teaspoon freshly ground black pepper

In a heavy saucepan, sauté the mushrooms and onion in olive oil over medium heat for about 7 minutes, or until the onion is translucent. Add the demi-glace and salt, bring to a boil, and then lower to simmer. Leave uncovered and simmer for about 20 minutes, or until the liquid has reduced by about one-third. Add the pepper and serve immediately, or store in an airtight container in the refrigerator for up to 7 days. This may also be frozen for up to 6 months.

MAKES 1½ CUPS

DEMI-GLACE
This may sound all French and daunting, but it's really easy and can be frozen in small containers for up to 3 months, so you can pull it out as needed. You can also purchase demi-glace in grocery stores and gourmet shops, of course, but we like the freshness of making it from scratch. In a heavy saucepan, heat 2 teaspoons olive oil and add 1 cup diced celery, 1 cup diced onion, and 1 cup diced carrots. Cook on high heat, stirring frequently with a wooden spoon, for about 10 minutes, or until caramelized. Add 1 cup dry red wine and cook uncovered over high heat for about 5 minutes, or until reduced by one-half. Add 4 cups beef stock and 2 tablespoons tomato paste. Stir together well, decrease the heat to medium, and simmer for about 25 minutes, or until reduced by one-quarter. Cool and refrigerate for up to 2 weeks.

Sunshot Farm

Our farm north of Asheville is situated in a fertile mountain valley, just west of the highest peak in the eastern United States, Mount Mitchell. We produce seasonal vegetables—from blueberries and tomatoes to leeks, squash, and lettuces. We don't grow enough to keep the restaurant completely satisfied, so we rely on our neighbor farmers and the abundance of fresh produce coming out of western North Carolina. What we do gain from being so close to the farm is a vital understanding of what's in season.

Tomato gravy is a Southern Appalachian tradition and a delicious alternative to cream-based gravies. It's an amazing accompaniment to breakfast eggs, meat loaf, grits, catfish, biscuits, fried chicken, and mashed potatoes.

TOMATO SHALLOT GRAVY

½ cup diced shallots (about 4 large shallots)

1 cup diced red onion (about 1 large onion)

1 tablespoon extra-virgin olive oil

1 cup canned plum tomatoes

1 cup demi-glace (page 13)

½ teaspoon sea salt

1½ teaspoons finely chopped fresh parsley

½ teaspoon freshly ground black pepper

In a thick-bottomed saucepan, sauté the shallots and onion in olive oil on medium heat for about 5 minutes, or until translucent. Add the tomatoes, breaking them into pieces with a wooden spoon, and the demi-glace and bring to a simmer. Add the salt and continue to simmer uncovered for about 20 minutes, or until reduced by one-third. Add the parsley and pepper and stir to combine. Serve immediately or cool and refrigerate in an airtight container for up to 3 days.

MAKES 2 CUPS

The Low Country is synonomous with coastal South Carolina and Georgia, where landed gentry typically sought out the coolness of the North Carolina mountains when summer became notoriously hot and humid. We still have lots of folks, many of whom have summer homes in the area, who come to Asheville from the heat of Charleston and environs. This rich gravy offers them a taste of home. It's delicious with grits and biscuits and as an accompaniment to mashed potatoes.

LOW COUNTRY GRAVY

2 slices good bacon, chopped into small pieces

4½ teaspoons all-purpose flour

2 cups heavy cream

⅛ teaspoon cayenne pepper

1 teaspoon minced fresh sage

½ teaspoon sea salt

¼ teaspoon freshly ground black pepper

In a thick-bottomed saucepan, brown the bacon on high heat, stirring occasionally, until browned. Reduce the heat to medium and add the flour, stirring constantly for 4 minutes, making a roux (see box). Add the cream, cayenne, sage, salt, and black pepper and continue cooking over medium to low heat for 5 to 7 minutes, stirring often, until thick and creamy. Serve immediately, or store in an airtight container in the refrigerator for up to 7 days.

MAKES APPROXIMATELY 2 CUPS

WHEN YOU WANT TO MAKE A ROUX
Making a roux is an important step in most French and Louisiana cooking, since it's a thickening concoction giving gumbo its mojo and creamy sauces their heft. Sauté 2 parts flour with 1 part canola oil over medium heat, stirring constantly, for about 5 minutes, or until it turns a blonde color. The mixture will be pasty in texture. Voilà!

This is one of those fancy touches to a meal when you want to impress your family and friends. The black truffle peelings can be purchased in gourmet shops or on specialty food Web sites. An interesting movement to cultivate truffles is currently under way in the mountains of Tennessee and North Carolina and is being met with some success. A fruity, earthy, and rich accompaniment, this sauce pairs well with beef, duck, and pork. Refrigerate in an airtight container for up to 1 week.

CHERRY TRUFFLE SAUCE

½ cup diced sweet onion (such as Vidalia)

½ cup peeled, diced carrots

½ cup diced celery

2 cups demi-glace (page 13)

½ cup dried cherries

1 tablespoon black truffle peelings

¼ teaspoon minced fresh thyme

¼ teaspoon minced fresh sage

In a heavy saucepan, combine the onion, carrots, celery, and demi-glace over high heat until the mixture begins to boil. Lower the heat to medium-low and simmer for about 20 minutes, or until reduced by about one-third. Strain off the vegetables and discard them, and return the sauce to the pan. Add the cherries, truffle peelings, thyme, and sage and stir well. Simmer for 5 minutes over medium heat before serving, or store in an airtight container in the refrigerator for up to 7 days. This sauce may also be frozen for up to 6 months.

MAKES 2 CUPS

We are lucky to live close enough to the coast to have fresh seafood delivered to our door year-round, and this sauce, with a great piece of just-caught grouper or sea bass, will brighten even the coldest January night or help you chill at a summer cookout. It's also great with grilled chicken.

ORANGE CILANTRO SAUCE

1 medium tomato

1 cup freshly squeezed orange juice (about 4 oranges)

¼ teaspoon sea salt

⅛ teaspoon ground white pepper

1 teaspoon minced fresh cilantro

1½ teaspoons unsalted butter

1 orange, peeled, seeded, and segmented

Core and halve the tomato. With a spoon, gently remove the seeds and squeeze out the juice. Cut the tomato into thin strips, about ¼ cup, and refrigerate the rest of the tomato in an airtight container for future use. Place the orange juice in a small saucepan and boil for about 5 minutes, or until the juice is reduced by half. Lower the heat to medium and add the salt, white pepper, tomato, and cilantro. Add the butter and stir constantly until melted. Remove from the heat and add the orange segments. Serve immediately.

MAKES 1½ CUPS

This is a zesty tomato-based sauce that's extremely versatile. We use it as the foundation for everything from enchilada sauce to spaghetti sauce. You can also make lots of it when fresh tomatoes are at their peak in the summertime and freeze it for those nippy fall and winter nights when you are longing for the taste of fresh tomato. Be sure you try it in making our Baked Goat Cheese and Smoked Tomato Dip with Garlic Crostini (page 51).

SMOKED TOMATO SAUCE

1 tablespoon olive oil

8 to 10 cloves garlic

½ cup diced sweet onion (such as Vidalia)

½ cup dry white wine

1 (8-ounce) can crushed tomatoes

1 (14-ounce) can whole peeled tomatoes

1 tablespoon tomato paste

½ cup water

1 cup smoked tomatoes, peeled (page 28), or canned fire-roasted tomatoes

1½ teaspoons minced fresh oregano

½ cup chopped fresh basil

½ teaspoon minced fresh thyme

1½ teaspoons sea salt

¼ tablespoon freshly ground black pepper

1 tablespoon plus 1½ teaspoons sugar

In a heavy saucepan, combine the olive oil, garlic, and onion over medium heat and sauté for about 5 minutes, or until the onion is translucent. Add the wine and turn the heat to high, cooking for 2 minutes. Add the crushed tomatoes, whole peeled tomatoes, tomato paste, water, smoked tomatoes, oregano, basil, thyme, salt, pepper, and sugar and bring to a boil. Reduce the heat to low and simmer, uncovered, for about 30 minutes, or until the mixture is reduced by one-fourth. Remove from the heat and puree in a food processor or blender. Serve immediately or cool and refrigerate in an airtight container for up to 14 days.

MAKES APPROXIMATELY 4 CUPS

In the South, the question of who makes the best 'cue is a debate we take very, very seriously. And no place more so than North Carolina, where the eastern part of the state avows a vinegar-based sauce while the western side vows tomato carries the day. Our basic sauce incorporates sorghum, a mountain staple, and root beer, just because. Actually, the root beer adds a hint of sassafras to the concoction. Traditional barbecue is pork centered, but this sauce is yummy with beef brisket or short ribs. We smoke our own peppers, but you can use La Costena or Contessa chipotle peppers in adobo. Just remember barbecue is a noun.

BASIC BARBECUE SAUCE

½ cup firmly packed light brown sugar

½ cup diced Vidalia onion

2 tablespoons roasted garlic puree (page 5)

½ cup cider vinegar

2 tablespoons Worcestershire sauce

2 cups ketchup

1 teaspoon hot pepper sauce

½ cup sorghum molasses

1 teaspoon freshly squeezed lemon juice

1 teaspoon sea salt

2 smoked jalapeño peppers, left whole (page 28)

1 teaspoon freshly ground black pepper

½ cup root beer

1 teaspoon chili powder

1 teaspoon ground cumin

1 teaspoon ground coriander

1 teaspoon dry mustard

Combine all the ingredients in a heavy saucepan or pot and bring to a boil over high heat. Reduce the heat to low and simmer for about 30 minutes, or until reduced by one-fourth. Allow to cool. Puree the sauce in a food processor before use. Refrigerate in an airtight container for up to 1 week.

MAKES 4 CUPS

Wings are ubiquitous during North Carolina college football and basketball games, but we think it's time to let these babies fly year-round, anytime, anywhere. We believe our sauce is just too good to place restrictions on when it's wing time. To each his own, we say, when it comes to hot pepper sauce, although our pick is Texas Pete. Despite its moniker, this delicious hot pepper sauce is made in North Carolina. If you don't smoke your own peppers, you can use Contessa smoked chipotle peppers in adobo.

TUPELO HONEY WING SAUCE

½ cup tupelo honey

2 tablespoons orange marmalade

¾ cup hot pepper sauce

1½ teaspoons smoked jalapeños (page 28)

1 teaspoon unsalted butter

Puree the honey, marmalade, hot pepper sauce, and jalapeños in a food processor until smooth. Transfer the mixture to a small saucepan over medium heat, bring to a simmer, and cook for 1 minute. Add the butter and stir until melted. Serve immediately or refrigerate in an airtight container for up to 2 weeks.

MAKES 1½ CUPS

We use this smoky sauce frequently, and so we make it in large batches and keep plenty on hand. We believe this melding of ingredients is the perfect blend of heat and sweet, and we love using real tupelo honey. You can use Contessa smoked chipotle peppers in adobo if you don't smoke your own peppers. But try smoking your own—it's fun.

SMOKED JALAPEÑO SAUCE

1 large jalapeño, smoked (page 28)

¼ cup orange marmalade

⅓ cup tupelo honey

½ cup freshly squeezed orange juice

½ cup V8 juice

1½ teaspoons chili powder

1½ teaspoons ground cumin

1½ teaspoons roasted garlic puree

¾ teaspoon ground coriander

⅛ teaspoon sea salt

1½ teaspoons cornstarch

1 tablespoon water

3 tablespoons freshly squeezed lime juice

1½ teaspoons minced fresh cilantro

Combine the smoked jalapeño, marmalade, honey, orange juice, V8 juice, chili powder, cumin, garlic puree, coriander, and salt in a large saucepan and bring to a boil over high heat. Combine the cornstarch and water in a small bowl and stir thoroughly. Decrease the heat to medium and add the cornstarch mixture to the saucepan with a whisk. Cook for 2 minutes, decrease the heat to low, and cook for about 5 minutes longer, or until the mixture coats the back of a spoon. Remove from the heat and strain the sauce through a fine-mesh sieve. Puree the cooked jalapeño in a food processor and add back to the sauce. Add the lime juice and cilantro. Refrigerate in an airtight container for up to 3 weeks.

MAKES 1½ CUPS

In the southern Appalachian mountains, we make sorghum molasses. In the old days, the cane was ground using a horse-drawn mill, and if you travel back into hollers and coves, you can still see this being practiced. You will see molasses made from sugarcane as well, but there's something about the earthiness of sorghum cane that makes this sauce taste like the Blue Ridge. Use it to anoint your grilled pork or chicken.

COFFEE MOLASSES
BARBECUE SAUCE

2 cups Basic Barbecue Sauce (page 21)

¾ cup sorghum molasses

1 cup brewed coffee

1 cup water

Combine all the ingredients in a heavy saucepan and bring to a boil. Lower the heat and simmer, uncovered, for about 40 minutes, or until reduced by about one-fourth. This can be stored in an airtight container in the refrigerator for up to 1 week.

MAKES 4½ CUPS

Two of our favorite ideas, joined together with pure simplicity. No wonder it sends us into orbit every time. This mixture can be used either as a marinade or brushed on as a grilling glaze for chicken, pork, or beef. And, as a bonus, stored in the refrigerator, the sauce is good for 1 month.

ROOT BEER–SORGHUM
MOLASSES GLAZE

1 (12-ounce) can root beer

⅓ cup sorghum molasses

Combine the root beer and molasses in a heavy saucepan and bring to a boil. Reduce the heat to medium and simmer for about 20 minutes, or until the mixture is reduced by about one-third.

MAKES ¾ CUP

Dressings and Spreads

Salads are a mixture of great raw ingredients coming together in a happy celebration, so dressings need to be fresh and bright, too. Think of them as the party guests who keep the conversation lively and fun. Or the drum circle, an impromptu group of spirited musicians drumming and dancing to the city's unique rhythms that happens every Friday night across the street from Tupelo.

Our tomato vinaigrette features our favorite jalapeño sauce. And we think our sweet and nutty Pecan Vinaigrette is a great foil to any salad greens but particularly to the swift bite of arugula and endive. Making your own salad dressings from scratch using fresh ingredients may add a step or two to dinner, but once you taste these, you'll kiss bottled dressing good-bye.

Don't skimp on the ingredients in this delicious and easy dressing—use good-quality olive oil, whole-grain mustard, fresh basil, and balsamic vinegar. Try it paired with our deliciously simple Southern Spring Salad with Basil Vinaigrette (page 91).

BASIL VINAIGRETTE

½ cup balsamic vinegar

2 cloves garlic, chopped

3 teaspoons diced Vidalia onion

⅛ teaspoon dry mustard

2 teaspoons Dijon mustard

2 teaspoons whole-grain mustard

½ teaspoon sugar

2 tablespoons finely chopped fresh basil

¼ teaspoon sea salt

¼ teaspoon freshly ground black pepper

1 cup canola oil

½ cup extra-virgin olive oil

Blend the vinegar, garlic, onion, dry mustard, Dijon mustard, whole-grain mustard, sugar, basil, salt, and pepper in a food processor. With the processor running, slowly drizzle in the canola oil followed by the olive oil until the mixture is thoroughly blended. Store in an airtight container in the refrigerator for up to 30 days.

MAKES 2 CUPS

Everyone knows that adding some hickory smoke when cooking meats on the grill or in the smoker is a good thing. So it stands to reason that smoking tomatoes would benefit in a similar way, right? This distinctive vinaigrette takes a little extra time, but everyone will want to know how you did it. Try it with your favorite mixed green salad topped with grilled chicken or shrimp.

SPICY SMOKED TOMATO
VINAIGRETTE

2 medium smoked tomatoes, peeled (see box)

⅓ cup Smoked Jalapeño Sauce (page 23)

¼ cup freshly squeezed lime juice

¼ teaspoon ground cumin

¼ teaspoon ground coriander

¼ teaspoon chili powder

¼ teaspoon sweet paprika

1 clove garlic, chopped

¼ cup minced fresh cilantro

½ teaspoon Dijon mustard

½ teaspoon whole-grain mustard

¼ cup cider vinegar

½ cup extra-virgin olive oil

Puree the tomatoes, jalapeño sauce, lime juice, cumin, coriander, chili powder, paprika, and garlic in a food processor. Add the cilantro, Dijon mustard, whole-grain mustard, and cider vinegar. While the machine is running, slowly drizzle in the olive oil until the mixture thickens. This dressing can be refrigerated in an airtight container for up to 1 week.

MAKES 1½ CUPS

SMOKED TOMATOES AND JALAPEÑOS
MAKES 2 CUPS

To smoke the tomatoes, put 2 cups hickory chips in the bottom of a 4-inch deep heavy roasting pan. Cover with water and let sit for 5 minutes. Drain the water and cover the chips with aluminum foil. Core 4 tomatoes and score the tops and bottoms with an X, using a sharp paring knife. Place the tomatoes on the foil, cover the pan tightly with additional foil, and put in a 450°F oven for about 10 minutes. (The foil will puff up like you're making Jiffy popcorn.) Turn the oven down to 250°F and cook for 20 to 30 minutes longer, until the tomatoes are slightly browned. Allow the tomatoes to cool before peeling. Refrigerate in an airtight container for up to 1 week. Makes 2 cups. We use the same process for smoking jalapeño peppers. Use whole peppers and remove the seeds and membranes after roasting and before storing in the refrigerator.

This creamy ranch dressing is fresh and simple and as easy as opening up a bottle of dressing but with twice the flavor. We love it with our Spinach Salad with Roasted Beets, Goat Cheese, Peppered Bacon, and Garlic Ranch Dressing (page 90).

GARLIC RANCH DRESSING

⅔ cup buttermilk

⅔ cup sour cream

⅔ cup mayonnaise

2 tablespoons chopped fresh parsley

2 tablespoons chopped fresh chives

3 tablespoons roasted garlic puree (optional if you want lots of garlic flavor)

1 clove garlic, minced

½ teaspoon sea salt

½ teaspoon freshly ground black pepper

Blend all the ingredients in a food processor for 30 seconds. Refrigerate for up to 10 days.

MAKES 2 CUPS

Toasting the pecans before adding them to the dressing brings out their amazingly sweet flavor. This vinaigrette is great on a traditional greens salad, but you should also try it with roasted vegetables such as green beans and beets. In our restaurant, it's a favorite accompaniment to our Peachy Grilled Chicken Salad with Pecan Vinaigrette (page 89).

PECAN VINAIGRETTE

¼ cup pecans

¼ cup cider vinegar

1 clove garlic, minced

2½ teaspoons Dijon mustard

2½ teaspoons whole-grain
    mustard

1 tablespoon plus 1½ teaspoons
    tupelo honey

2 teaspoons sugar

1 teaspoon sea salt

1 teaspoon freshly ground
    black pepper

1 cup canola oil

¼ cup extra-virgin olive oil

Roast the pecans on a rimmed sheet pan in a 350°F oven for about 20 minutes, or until the pecans are roasted or slightly browned. Remove, cool, and grind in a food processor until the mixture resembles coarse cornmeal. Transfer the pecans to a small bowl. Puree the vinegar, garlic, Dijon mustard, whole-grain mustard, honey, sugar, salt, and pepper in a food processor and while the machine is running, drizzle in the canola oil and olive oil. Remove and pour into a container. Stir in the ground pecans and serve. Store in an airtight container in the refrigerator for up to 30 days.

MAKES 2 CUPS

Pictured top to bottom: Creamy Maple Mustard Dressing, Raspberry Honey Mayonaise, and Cherry Apple Chowchow.

This is where the South meets Vermont. At Tupelo, we always use Duke's mayonnaise. If you can't find it, you can actually order it online at www.boiledpeanuts.com, a Web site developed by friends, cookbook authors, and brothers Matt and Ted Lee to quench the cravings of ex-pat Southerners. It tastes like homemade mayo, so if you know how to make your own mayonnaise, you can do that, too. The maple syrup lends just the right touch of mellow sweetness. Try it on a warm sweet potato salad or as an accompaniment to roast beef or grilled chicken sandwiches. Refrigerate for up to 1 week.

CREAMY MAPLE
MUSTARD DRESSING

1½ cups mayonnaise

¼ cup pure maple syrup

2 tablespoons cider vinegar

2 tablespoons Dijon mustard

2 tablespoons whole-grain
   mustard

¼ teaspoon sea salt

¼ teaspoon freshly ground
   black pepper

Combine all the ingredients with a whisk in a large bowl. Refrigerate for at least 2 hours before serving. Store refrigerated for up to 7 days.

MAKES 2 CUPS

Fresh basil is fragrant with hints of anise and pairs delectably with the sweetness of cashews in this pesto with a twist. Serve tossed with pasta, spread on crostini as an appetizer, or paired with grilled chicken and fish. It's also fantastic with raw vegetables as a crudités partner.

BASIL CASHEW PESTO

½ cup firmly packed fresh basil

⅓ cup roasted, salted cashews

2 cloves garlic

1 tablespoon freshly squeezed lemon juice

⅛ teaspoon sea salt

⅛ teaspoon freshly ground black pepper

⅓ cup extra-virgin olive oil

Combine the basil, cashews, garlic, lemon juice, salt, and pepper in a food processor. Drizzle the olive oil into the mixture and blend until smooth. Serve immediately or refrigerate in an airtight container for up to 1 week.

MAKES ½ CUP

RASPBERRY HONEY
MAYONNAISE

- 1 tablespoon mayonnaise
- 2 teaspoons raspberry preserves
- 1 teaspoon tupelo honey
- ¼ teaspoon sea salt
- ¼ teaspoon freshly ground black pepper

Using a wire whisk, combine all the ingredients in a small bowl. Refrigerate in a covered container for up to 1 week. This is delicious on turkey sandwiches and particularly with our Grilled Club Sandwich with Brie and Raspberry Honey Mayonnaise (page 71).

MAKES 1 SERVING

CRANBERRY MAYONNAISE

- 2 tablespoons canned whole cranberry dressing
- 2 tablespoons good-quality mayonnaise

Combine the cranberry dressing and mayonnaise in a bowl, using a wire whisk. This spread is wonderful on sandwiches, especially our Tupelo Honey Chicken Sandwich with Havarti Cheese and Cranberry Mayonnaise (page 76).

MAKES 1 SERVING

Wake up your ham sandwiches! Shake up your grilled cheese! Agitate your egg salad! This yummy mayonnaise will keep refrigerated for 2 weeks so you can experiment.

SMOKED JALAPEÑO AIOLI

½ cup good-quality mayonnaise

2 tablespoons Smoked Jalapeño Sauce (page 23)

1 teaspoon freshly squeezed lemon juice

⅛ teaspoon sea salt

⅛ teaspoon freshly ground black pepper

Combine all the ingredients in a medium bowl with a fine wire whisk until thoroughly blended. Serve immediately, or store in an airtight container in the refrigerator for up to 14 days.

MAKES ¾ CUP

Preserves and Pickles

Every Appalachian cook knows the importance of thinking ahead to winter when your taste buds are longing for some flavor of the farm. Drying, salting and curing, canning and preserving, and pickling were all originally children of necessity, the result of needing to prepare for long winters in the coves and hollers of the Blue Ridge. Now, we just like the way the vinegary sweetness and tartness of chowchow (a pickled-cabbage cousin of kraut with some sweetness and varying degrees of heat) or the fragrance of fruity preserves makes something otherwise good into something great. Case in point is our Cherry Apple Chowchow (page 39), which is a sort of marriage of the two ideas.

We also get lots of requests for our Peach Butter, probably because it's mainly peaches and butter and sugar and, well, how could anything be better? Unless it's Blackberry Skillet Jam. Simple and simply amazing. You can find pectin in the baking or canning section of your grocery store.

The North Carolina mountains offer the ideal growing spot for blueberries, which grow wild on many local mountain knobs and balds. We have one thousand bushes on our farm, which help keep us in the glory of blueberries year-round. Chef Brian has been known, in fact, to throw the occasional summertime blueberry feast, featuring all manner of blueberry dishes. These preserves can be used as a simple sauce that is delicious over roasted duck, tucked into Tupelo Honey Ginormous Biscuits (page 189), or drizzled on hot pancakes.

BLUEBERRY PRESERVES

¾ cup sugar

1½ teaspoons pectin

4 cups fresh blueberries (about 1½ pounds)

1 tablespoon freshly squeezed lemon juice

Combine the sugar and pectin in a large bowl until thoroughly blended. Place the blueberries in a medium saucepan and stir in the sugar mixture and lemon juice. Bring to a boil, reduce the heat to medium, and cook, occasionally stirring, for about 10 minutes, or until the mixture coats the back of a spoon. Allow to cool to room temperature before serving. Store in an airtight container for up to 30 days.

MAKES 2¼ CUPS

Blackberries grow with wild abandon throughout the southern Appalachian region and ripen to sheer bliss in the hotter months of July and August. In fact, combining berry picking with a mountain hike is a favorite pastime for locals and visitors alike. If you don't have time to make jam or jelly the old-fashioned way, here's a recipe that will make your biscuit happy.

BLACKBERRY SKILLET JAM

1 cup sugar

4 teaspoons pectin

4 cups fresh blackberries
(about 1½ pounds)

4 teaspoons freshly squeezed
lemon juice

Combine the sugar and pectin in a medium bowl and mix thoroughly. Put the berries in a heavy saucepan or skillet and add the sugar mixture. Add the lemon juice and put on high heat until simmering. Reduce the heat to medium and continue to simmer, stirring occasionally, for about 10 minutes, or until the mixture coats the back of a spoon. Refrigerate for up to 2 weeks.

MAKES 3 CUPS

This chowchow is really a beauty. Its brilliant color is outdone only by its zingy sweet-and-sour taste. We favor it on homemade Reuben sandwiches with either turkey, pastrami, or corned beef. But you can also serve it with roast pork or grilled chicken. Just stand back while the compliments fly.

CHERRY APPLE CHOWCHOW

3 tablespoons dried cherries

1 cup coarsely chopped dried apples (about 8 ounces dried apples)

2 cups shredded red cabbage (1 small head red cabbage)

1 small Vidalia onion, diced

½ cup water

¼ cup cider vinegar

¼ cup orange marmalade

1 tablespoon Dijon mustard

1 tablespoon whole-grain mustard

Combine all the ingredients in a heavy saucepan and bring to a boil. Reduce the heat and simmer for about 25 minutes, or until the liquid evaporates by one-half. Refrigerate overnight in an airtight container. The chowchow will keep for up to 1 week.

MAKES 2 CUPS

Peaches are arguably the perfect fruit—sweet, juicy, flavorful, rich in vitamins and nutrients. And when they are at their height of ripeness in the summer, they taste like summer itself. Tupelo is in wonderful proximity to South Carolina and Georgia, both robust producers of the peach. But you can also use frozen peaches if fresh are not available. At the restaurant, our peach butter is famously served with our decadent Sweet Potato Pancakes (page 199).

PEACH BUTTER

8 tablespoons unsalted butter, at room temperature

1 large ripe peach, peeled and finely diced, or ¾ cup frozen peaches, diced fine

1½ teaspoons brown sugar

⅛ teaspoon sea salt

1 tablespoon peach nectar

In a food processor, combine all the ingredients by pulsing briefly, retaining pieces of peach visible in the mixture. Keep refrigerated, but bring it to room temperature before serving. Try it on hot biscuits, cornbread, or waffles.

MAKES 1 CUP

Southerners love pickles as a delicious and easy way to put up fruits and vegetables at the end of harvest—pickled peaches, pickled okra, pickled watermelon rind, pickled beans. We even pickle eggs. We are also crazy about the idea of savory married with sweet. Use sweet Vidalia onions in this recipe for the best results. These pickles are delicious with roasted fish or as a condiment for warm grilled chicken or roast beef sandwiches.

PICKLED SWEET ONIONS

1 large Vidalia onion, sliced into ¼-inch rings

4 tablespoons sugar

4 tablespoons cider vinegar

¼ teaspoon sea salt

¼ teaspoon freshly ground black pepper

1 cup water

In a heavy saucepan, combine all the ingredients and bring to a boil. Decrease the heat to medium and simmer uncovered for about 30 minutes, or until the onion is translucent. Remove from the heat, cool, and put in an airtight container. Refrigerate for at least 2 hours before serving. The pickled onions may be refrigerated for up to 2 weeks.

MAKES ½ CUP

Asheville City Market c. 1920

ANGELS OF THE FIRST DEGREE:
HEAVENLY APPETIZERS AND SOUPS

APPETIZERS

Crispy Fried Artichokes with
Oven-Roasted Tomatoes
and Lemon Vinaigrette

Baked Goat Cheese and Smoked
Tomato Dip with Garlic Crostini

Nut-Crusted Brie with Cabernet
Balsamic–Glazed Figs

Warm Pimento Cheese
and Chips

Mushroom Quesadilla with
Green Tomato Salsa and
Smoked Jalapeño Sauce

Tupelo Honey Wings

Cheesy Grits Cakes with
Sunshot Salsa and Smoked
Jalapeño Sauce

SOUPS

Creamy Tomato Soup

Cheesy Onion Bisque

Carolina Fish Chowder

Coconut Sweet Potato Bisque

Corn and Crab Chowder

We believe appetizers and soups are a lot like a first date. You want to make a good impression, leaving your date hungry for more when you say good night. You don't want to overwhelm him with too much makeup or perfume or big hair. You want to be sure she thinks you look cool and hip but also accessible and approachable. You want to stand out as different from others, but you don't want to overthink it and botch up what's organically, genuinely *already there*.

So we start with the natural goodness we've been given and simply try to present it with our own singularly Tupelo Honey Cafe flair. We want to appreciate our earthly assets first and foremost before we dress them for dinner.

One of our favorite experiences in the restaurant involves watching folks order several appetizers as a way to share with one another. It's a wonderfully convivial way to commune and something of an Asheville tradition. Across town at Biltmore House in the late 1800s, George Vanderbilt entertained family and friends with elaborate twelve-course dinners. You can bet appetizers and soups were on those menus. And during author Thomas Wolfe's boyhood in the 1930s, his mother, Julia, ran their boardinghouse just a few blocks from Tupelo Honey—where passing plates of food would have been a nightly event.

The point is, our community has long been fortunate in attracting colorful personalities and visionaries, many of whom left their mark clearly on Asheville. These first fathers and mothers were early influencers, helping shape our collective character as a city and leaving both first and lasting impressions behind. Their spirits are often felt here as we gather friends and families around our tables, as we toast the magic of sharing good food and drink as confirmation that you can, in fact, *always* go home again.

"She's as sweet as tupelo honey. She's an angel of the first degree."

—Van Morrison

Appetizers

Put on your best mixologist hat, pull out the serving platters, and get ready to entertain with ease. Serving appetizers and cocktails before dinner is a terrific way to welcome your guests and get the conversation started. If you want to have a fun, informal gathering, invite the crowd over for an appetizer and drinks only get-together and toast, mingle, and nosh.

Go ahead and indulge a little. Go in the kitchen, put on your apron, and turn on some Ella Fitzgerald. Sing along. Then impress everyone with this fantastic, classic combination of flavors. The dressing is a delicious addition to just about any fresh green salad. Serve with crusty bread.

CRISPY FRIED ARTICHOKES WITH OVEN-ROASTED TOMATOES AND LEMON VINAIGRETTE

4 cups canola oil

1 cup all-purpose flour

3 tablespoons cornstarch

1 teaspoon sea salt

1 teaspoon freshly ground black pepper

2 (12-ounce) cans artichoke hearts, drained (about 20 artichokes)

Oven-Roasted Tomatoes (recipe follows)

Salad greens

Lemon Vinaigrette (recipe follows)

Heat the canola oil in a heavy saucepan over medium heat until it reaches 350°F, or is beginning to bubble. In a small bowl, combine the flour, cornstarch, salt, and pepper. Coat each artichoke heart in the flour mixture. With a slotted spoon, fry the artichokes in the hot oil for 3 to 4 minutes, until golden brown. Drain well on paper towels. Place the artichokes and the tomatoes on top of the salad greens and drizzle with the vinaigrette.

MAKES 4 SERVINGS

 Kölsch

Sangiovese or Pinot Grigio

OVEN-ROASTED TOMATOES

¼ cup balsamic vinegar

¼ cup extra-virgin olive oil

½ teaspoon plus ⅛ teaspoon sea salt

½ teaspoon plus ⅛ teaspoon freshly ground black pepper

12 Roma tomatoes, cut in half lengthwise

⅛ teaspoon dried thyme

⅛ teaspoon dried oregano

Fresh thyme or oregano leaves, for garnish

Preheat the oven to 350°F. In a large bowl, whisk together the balsamic vinegar, olive oil, ½ teaspoon of the sea salt, and ½ teaspoon of the pepper. Add the tomatoes to the mixture and toss gently until the tomatoes are coated. Place a wire rack on top of a rimmed sheet pan and place the tomatoes cut side up on top of the wire rack, reserving the vinaigrette mixture. In a small bowl, combine the remaining ⅛ teaspoon salt and ⅛ teaspoon pepper, the thyme, and oregano. Sprinkle the herb mixture on top of the tomatoes and place the sheet pan in the oven for about 1 hour, or until just beginning to caramelize. Remove the pan from the oven and brush the tomatoes with the reserved vinaigrette, using a pastry brush. Continue to cook for about 30 minutes longer, or until lightly browned. Remove from the oven and cool to room temperature. Garnish.

MAKES 24 TOMATO HALVES; 6 SERVINGS

LEMON VINAIGRETTE

1 tablespoon shallots, finely minced

2 cloves garlic, finely minced

⅛ teaspoon dried oregano

⅛ teaspoon sea salt

⅛ teaspoon freshly ground black pepper

3 tablespoons freshly squeezed lemon juice

1 tablespoon sherry vinegar

1 teaspoon minced fresh basil

½ teaspoon sugar

½ cup extra-virgin olive oil

Place the shallots, garlic, oregano, salt, pepper, lemon juice, vinegar, basil, and sugar in a food processor and blend well. While the machine is running, slowly drizzle in the olive oil to thicken.

MAKES ¾ CUP

"At the midday meal, they ate heavily: a huge hot roast of beef, fat buttered lima-beans, tender corn smoking on the cob, thick red slabs of sliced tomatoes, rough savory spinach, hot yellow corn-bread, flaky biscuits, a deep-dish peach and apple cobbler spiced with cinnamon, tender cabbage, deep glass dishes piled with preserved fruits—cherries, pears, peaches."

—Asheville author Thomas Wolfe, from *Look Homeward, Angel*

On Coming Home

Author Thomas Wolfe is Asheville's best-known writer. Born here in 1900, he is considered one of the important major American novelists of the early twentieth century. His prominent works include *Look Homeward, Angel* and *You Can't Go Home Again*, both works including thinly veiled autobiographical references and recognizable Asheville citizens, many of whom weren't pleased with his depictions of them during his lifetime. His childhood home on Spruce Street, where his mother ran a boarding-house called "Old Kentucky Home," is open to the public for tours. Wolfe is pictured above with his mother, Julia, in 1937.

Western North Carolina has several outstanding artisanal goat cheese makers and many of them make out-of-this-world cheeses—rosemary fig goat cheese, dill goat cheese, roasted garlic goat cheese. Use regular goat cheese (is there really such a thing?) in this recipe. This full-flavored cheese with a tangy touch pairs deliciously with smoked tomatoes.

BAKED GOAT CHEESE AND SMOKED TOMATO DIP WITH GARLIC CROSTINI

1 cup Smoked Tomato Sauce (page 20)

2 (4-ounce) logs goat cheese

¼ cup thinly sliced basil leaves

24 garlic crostini, for serving (recipe follows)

Preheat the oven to 400°F. Pour the smoked tomato sauce into a 4-cup casserole. Place the goat cheese logs in the center of the sauce and bake for about 20 minutes, or until the sauce and the cheese are heated through. Sprinkle with the basil leaves and serve immediately with the garlic crostini.

GARLIC CROSTINI

1 (16-inch) baguette

Roasted garlic oil (page 5)

½ teaspoon sea salt

½ teaspoon freshly ground black pepper

Preheat the oven to 400°F. Cut the baguette into 24 (¼-inch) slices. Place the baguette slices on a rimmed sheet pan and drizzle with the garlic oil. Sprinkle with the salt and pepper and place in the oven for 8 to 10 minutes, until browned. Remove from the oven and set aside to cool.

MAKES 4 SERVINGS

A richly satisfying combination of sweetness and creaminess, crowned with a hint of salty nuttiness, this is a lovely appetizer anytime, but it seems to fit especially well with fall and winter holidays and celebrations. It's also delicious paired with roast pork or lamb chops.

NUT-CRUSTED BRIE WITH CABERNET BALSAMIC–GLAZED FIGS

2 cups mixed roasted, salted nuts

2 cups panko bread crumbs

2 eggs

2 tablespoons half-and-half

1 cup all-purpose flour

3 (8-ounce) Brie wheels

3 Granny Smith apples, cored and seeded

1 teaspoon unsalted butter

2 cups Cabernet Balsamic–Glazed Figs (recipe follows)

2 cups canola oil

Garlic Crostini (page 51)

Combine the nuts and bread crumbs in a food processor and grind thoroughly. Transfer to a large bowl and set aside. In a medium bowl, whisk together the eggs and half-and-half to create an egg wash. Place the flour in a third bowl. Cut the Brie into 4 wedges per wheel to total 12 wedges. Dip the Brie wedges in the flour, then the egg wash, and finally the nut mixture. Repeat until all the wedges are coated and set aside.

Trim the top and bottom off each apple so the apple is flat on each end. Slice the apples sideways in half to make 6 round disks, each about 2 inches thick. In a large sauté pan or skillet, melt the butter over medium heat and add the apples. Cook 3 to 4 minutes on each side, until golden brown. Remove the pan from the heat, keeping the apples warm.

To assemble the dish, warm the Cabernet balsamic figs over low heat, just until warm, about 5 minutes. Heat the canola oil in a deep saucepan over medium heat until the oil is 325°F, or just bubbling. Add the Brie to the hot oil and cook for about 1 minute, or until softened and golden brown. Drain the wedges on paper towels. Place the apple rings on a serving platter, topping each ring with 2 Brie wedges. Top with the warm fig mixture and serve with the crostini.

MAKES 6 SERVINGS

CABERNET BALSAMIC–GLAZED FIGS

2 cups dried figs, stemmed and
    cut into quarters

1½ cups Cabernet Sauvignon

3 tablespoons balsamic vinegar

⅛ teaspoon sea salt

1 bay leaf

⅛ teaspoon freshly ground
    black pepper

2 teaspoons whole mustard
    seeds

½ teaspoon cornstarch

3 tablespoons cold water

In an 8-cup saucepan, combine the figs, wine, vinegar, salt, and bay leaf. Bring to a boil, immediately reduce to medium-low heat, and simmer, stirring frequently, for about 20 minutes, or until the mixture begins to slightly thicken. Add the pepper and mustard seeds and continue to simmer for 3 to 5 minutes longer. In a small bowl, combine the cornstarch and water and add this mixture to the figs. Simmer about 5 minutes, or until the mixture is the consistency of preserves, and remove from the heat. Transfer the figs to a covered container and cool in the refrigerator for at least 2 hours before serving.

MAKES 6 SERVINGS

🍺 **Belgian kriek ale**

🍷 **Cabernet Sauvignon**

Often called the pâté of the South, pimento cheese has as many variations as there are home cooks in the region. Many recipes are very specific when it comes to ingredients: one may require Duke's mayonnaise; another may demand only oven-roasted red bell peppers. One of our favorite Southern chefs spikes his pimento cheese with a touch of bourbon. Our PC is different because we serve it warm and with our homemade tortilla chips. Call it what you wish. We call it yummy.

WARM PIMENTO CHEESE AND CHIPS

8 ounces cheddar cheese, shredded

½ cup mayonnaise

1 tablespoon Dijon mustard

1 tablespoon stone-ground mustard

1 teaspoon mustard powder

¼ teaspoon sea salt

¼ teaspoon freshly ground black pepper

2 tablespoons minced fresh parsley

½ cup finely diced roasted red bell pepper

Tortilla chips, for serving

Combine the cheese, mayonnaise, Dijon mustard, stone-ground mustard, mustard powder, salt, pepper, parsley, and roasted bell peppers in a large bowl. Transfer to a microwavable dish and microwave for about 20 seconds, or until hot. Or put in a baking dish in a preheated 350°F oven for about 15 minutes, or until heated through. Serve with the tortilla chips.

MAKES 2 CUPS

 Pilsner

unoaked Chardonnay

Foraging for wild mushrooms in the Blue Ridge Mountains is a favorite pastime for many area mycologists, and morels, lobster oysters, hen of the woods, and chanterelles are readily available if you know where to look and what to look for. The accomplished mushroom hunter also knows which mountain mushrooms are poisonous, an understandably important piece of knowledge to have. Fortunately, you don't have to hunt your own mushrooms. Most grocery stores today carry a wide variety, certainly the ones we suggest here. Feel free to mix your mushroom types, however, to your heart's content.

MUSHROOM QUESADILLA WITH GREEN TOMATO SALSA AND SMOKED JALAPEÑO SAUCE

MUSHROOM MIXTURE

1 tablespoon unsalted butter

1 large Vidalia onion, chopped

2 cups oyster mushrooms, trimmed (about 8 ounces)

⅔ cup diced roasted red bell pepper

½ cup shiitake mushrooms, stems discarded and caps diced

1 teaspoon minced fresh thyme

1 teaspoon minced fresh sage

1 teaspoon minced fresh oregano

1 teaspoon sea salt

1 teaspoon freshly ground black pepper

1 teaspoon unsalted butter, at room temperature

6 (10-inch) flour tortillas

2 cups shredded sharp cheddar cheese (8 ounces)

⅓ cup Green Tomato Salsa (page 7)

⅓ cup sour cream

¼ cup Smoked Jalapeño Sauce (page 23)

Scottish ale

Cabernet Sauvignon

To make the mushroom mixture, melt the butter in a sauté pan or skillet and add the onion, cooking over medium heat, stirring occasionally, for about 10 minutes, or until caramelized. Add the oyster mushrooms, mushrooms, and bell pepper and continue cooking on medium heat for 5 minutes longer. Add the thyme, sage, oregano, salt, and pepper and stir for about 2 minutes. Remove from the heat and set aside.

Lightly spread the butter over 1 side of each tortilla. Place a tortilla, one at a time, butter side down, in a nonstick skillet over medium heat. Top the tortilla with ⅓ cup of the cheese and ⅔ cup of the mushroom mixture. Cook over medium heat for 2 minutes, or until lightly browned. With a rubber spatula, fold the tortilla in half and cook over medium heat for 2 minutes before carefully flipping the tortilla and cooking 2 minutes longer, or until lightly browned. Remove the quesadilla from the heat and plate on a serving platter, keeping warm until all the quesadilla have been cooked. Cut the quesadillas into quarters and garnish with the salsa, sour cream, and jalapeño sauce.

MAKES 6 SERVINGS

We've tried many (Chef Brian claims thousands) different preparations for chicken wings over the years and believe this is perfection. These are mandatory when ACC football or Carolina or Duke basketball season is under way. Our wing sauce is an important component and worth the extra effort.

TUPELO HONEY WINGS

4 cups canola oil

20 fresh chicken wings

4 cups freshly squeezed orange juice

4 cups water

1½ cups Tupelo Honey Wing Sauce (page 22)

Blue cheese salad dressing, for serving

Heat the canola oil in a large stockpot or deep fryer over medium heat until a deep-fat thermometer registers 350°F. In another large pot, combine the wings, orange juice, and water and bring to a boil. Boil the wings for about 10 minutes, or until the wings are cooked through and no longer pink when pierced or to a temperature of 160°F. Transfer the wings with a slotted spoon to paper towels and pat dry. Using a slotted spoon, carefully add the wings to the oil and fry for about 10 minutes, or until crispy golden brown. While the wings are frying, pour the wing sauce into a saucepan and bring just to a simmer. Remove the wings from the oil and drain on paper towels. Place the wings in a large bowl and add the sauce, stirring until well coated. Transfer the wings to a serving platter and serve with the dressing.

MAKES 20 WINGS

 Scottish ale or American amber ale

AIR

The Asheville Independent Restaurant Association began in 2000 as a volunteer organization but has since grown into a culinary tour de force with over 250 independent restaurants in the area. The group promotes the importance of supporting independent restaurants and the flavor they each bring to the community. Tupelo Honey Cafe is proud to be an active member of AIR.

Grits are such iconic Southern fare, rooted in our region's dependence on corn before processed wheat flour was widely available. If you're using true stone-ground grits, rather than instant, they are worth the trouble, if you can find them. These stone-ground grits require constant stirring over low heat for about 45 minutes, or until thick and creamy. If you're feeling creative, pour your hot grits mixture into a shallow casserole or rimmed sheet pan before refrigerating. Once set, use a cookie cutter to make grits cakes in your favorite shape.

CHEESY GRITS CAKES WITH SUNSHOT SALSA AND SMOKED JALAPEÑO SAUCE

2 cups water

½ teaspoon sea salt

1 tablespoon unsalted butter

1 cup quick grits or stone-ground grits

2 tablespoons heavy cream

¼ teaspoon freshly ground black pepper

1 cup shredded sharp cheddar cheese (about 4 ounces)

2 cups canola oil

3 cups white cornmeal

⅓ cup sour cream, for serving

Sunshot Salsa, for serving (page 8)

Smoked Jalapeño Sauce, for serving (page 23)

Lightly butter an 8-inch square casserole dish. Bring the water, salt, and butter to a boil in a heavy saucepan. Whisk in the grits and return to a boil. Reduce the heat to low and whisk in the cream. For quick grits, cook for 4 to 5 minutes, until thick and creamy. If you are using true grits, stir constantly over low heat for about 45 minutes, or until thick and creamy. Remove the grits from the heat and stir in the pepper and cheese until the cheese is melted and thoroughly combined. Pour the grits into the prepared casserole dish, cover, and refrigerate overnight.

Invert the casserole over a cutting surface and remove the grits from the pan. The grits should be set and solid. Cut the grits in half and then cut each half into 1-inch slices. Heat the canola oil in a sauté pan or skillet over medium heat until the oil is at 350°F on a deep-fat thermometer, or just boiling. Dredge the grit cakes in the cornmeal and add to the oil, cooking about 3 minutes on each side, or until golden brown and hot through the center. Serve with the sour cream, salsa, and jalapeño sauce.

MAKES 6 SERVINGS

Scottish ale

Petite Syrah or oaked Chardonnay

Tupelo Honey Cafe, South Asheville location

Soups

Strangely, some folks think of soup as a way to use leftovers. At Tupelo Honey, we believe flavorful, nourishing soup is one of the finest things in life, especially on a crisp fall evening or a cool summer night. Our soups are good introductions to larger menus, but there's nothing leftover about them, and they are delicious as the main attraction.

A real crowd pleaser, this rosy soup is great in the autumn and winter because it's delicious using canned tomatoes. The cream adds an elegant touch. Serve it with toast points or chips slathered with Warm Pimento Cheese (page 55). And have a bottle of hot sauce on hand if folks want a little more kick.

CREAMY TOMATO SOUP

1 (24-ounce) can crushed tomatoes, undrained

3 cups water

2 tablespoons tomato paste

1 bay leaf

2 teaspoons sugar

1½ teaspoons sea salt

½ teaspoon freshly ground black pepper

1 cup heavy cream

Combine the tomatoes, water, tomato paste, bay leaf, sugar, and salt in a 4-cup heavy saucepan. Bring to a boil, immediately decrease the heat to medium, and simmer for about 20 minutes, or until the mixture lightly coats the spoon. Whisk in the pepper and cream and continue cooking over medium heat for about 2 minutes, or until thoroughly blended.

MAKES 6 TO 8 SERVINGS

 Pilsner

Sangiovese

Two ingredients make this a favorite: onions and cheese. Vidalia onions are key here for their amazing sweetness. And we use three different cheeses plus cream to create this velvety smooth taste of heaven. It needs nothing more than our Southern Spring Salad with Basil Vinaigrette (page 91) or a Fried Green Tomato and Grilled Portobello Sandwich with Basil and Roasted Red Pepper Mayonnaise (page 79) to qualify as a feast.

CHEESY ONION BISQUE

2 tablespoons unsalted butter

3 large Vidalia onions, chopped

2 tablespoons all-purpose flour

5 cups chicken stock

1½ teaspoons sea salt

1 cup heavy cream

1 cup shredded Swiss cheese (about 4 ounces)

¼ cup shredded cheddar cheese

¼ cup grated fresh Parmesan cheese

1½ teaspoons freshly ground black pepper

In a 4-quart saucepan, melt the butter over medium-low heat and add the onions. Sauté, stirring often with a wooden spoon, for about 20 minutes, or until golden brown. Add the flour and continue stirring for 4 to 5 minutes, until thickened. Add the stock and bring to a boil, then decrease the heat to medium; add the salt and let simmer for about 15 minutes, or until the mixture coats the back of a spoon. Increase the heat to high and stir in the cream, cooking for about 5 minutes longer, or until the mixture is thick and creamy. Remove from the heat and add the Swiss cheese, cheddar cheese, Parmesan cheese, and pepper, whisking the mixture until the cheeses are completely melted. Serve immediately.

MAKES 6 TO 8 SERVINGS

 Weissbier

Petite Syrah

At Tupelo Honey, we are fortunate to receive frequent ocean bounty from our Carolina coastal fishermen. This hearty chowder can be made with almost any firm white fish, but our favorites are grouper, red snapper, and mahimahi. Make a skillet of cornbread and you're done.

CAROLINA FISH CHOWDER

1½ tablespoons unsalted butter

1 tablespoon vegetable oil

1 cup diced Vidalia onion (about 1 large onion)

1 cup diced celery (about 4 ribs)

1 cup peeled, diced carrots (about 2 medium carrots)

2 cups diced red potatoes (about 3 large potatoes)

1 bay leaf

1 (28-ounce) can diced tomatoes, including juice

3½ cups water

½ teaspoon Old Bay Seasoning

½ teaspoon dried thyme

½ teaspoon dried oregano

1 tablespoon sea salt

1 pound firm white fish, cut into bite-size pieces

1½ teaspoons freshly ground black pepper

Melt the butter in the vegetable oil in a 4-quart saucepan over high heat and sauté the onion, celery, carrots, and potatoes for about 5 minutes, or until the potatoes begin to be tender. Add the bay leaf, tomatoes, water, Old Bay Seasoning, thyme, oregano, and salt. Decrease the heat to medium and simmer for about 15 minutes, or until the mixture is heated through and the potatoes are fork tender. Add the fish and continue to simmer for about 10 minutes longer, or until the fish is cooked through and firm, being careful not to overcook so the fish retains its firmness. Add the pepper and serve immediately. This soup is delicious reheated the next day when all the flavors have melded.

MAKES 8 SERVINGS

German Weissbier or Belgian Witbier

Sauvignon Blanc

If you love sweet potatoes the way we do, you'll find this wonderfully fragrant soup addictive. The addition of coconut, milk, honey, and maple syrup elevate this lovely, aromatic bisque to dessert in a soup bowl. It's a wonderful partner with a savory sandwich, too, such as our Tupelo Honey Chicken Sandwich with Havarti Cheese and Cranberry Mayonnaise (page 76).

COCONUT SWEET POTATO BISQUE

2 large sweet potatoes, peeled and sliced

4 cups plus 4½ teaspoons water

1 (14-ounce) can unsweetened coconut milk

1 tablespoon brown sugar

1½ teaspoons pure maple syrup

1½ teaspoons tupelo honey

2½ teaspoons sea salt

¼ teaspoon pumpkin pie spice

½ teaspoon freshly ground black pepper

4½ teaspoons cornstarch

⅛ teaspoon cayenne pepper

In a 4-quart saucepan, combine the sweet potatoes and 4 cups of the water over high heat, bring to a boil, and boil for about 20 minutes, or until the potatoes are tender. Reduce the heat to medium and, using a potato masher, mash the potatoes in the water. Add the coconut milk, brown sugar, maple syrup, honey, salt, pumpkin pie spice, and black pepper and simmer for about 15 minutes, or until it begins to thicken. In a small bowl, combine the cornstarch and the remaining 4½ teaspoons water to form a thick paste. Add the cornstarch mixture and the cayenne to the soup and cook over low heat for about 5 minutes longer, or until it coats the back of a spoon. Use a handheld blender to puree the soup until smooth, or use a stand blender or food processor, working in batches, and transfer the soup back to the saucepan to keep warm.

MAKES 6 TO 8 SERVINGS

Belgian saison

gewurztraminer

This soup is good anytime but is particularly delicious in the summer, when fresh corn and crab are in abundance in the Carolinas. If you use frozen corn, choose white shoepeg.

CORN AND CRAB CHOWDER

4 strips bacon, diced

1 tablespoon unsalted butter

1 cup diced celery (about 4 ribs)

1 cup diced sweet onion (such as Vidalia; about 1 large onion)

1 cup diced red potato, unpeeled (about 3 potatoes)

3 tablespoons all-purpose flour

5 cups 2% milk

1 teaspoon minced fresh thyme

2 cups corn, cut from 3 to 4 large ears, or frozen

1 tablespoon sea salt

3 ounces claw crabmeat, picked free of shell

2 cups heavy cream

1 teaspoon freshly ground black pepper

¼ teaspoon hot pepper sauce

In a 4-quart saucepan, brown the bacon over medium heat until crispy. Remove with a slotted spoon and set aside to drain on paper towels. Add the butter to the bacon drippings and return to medium heat. Sauté the celery, onion, and potato in the butter mixture, stirring occasionally, for about 10 minutes, or until the vegetables are just tender and the onion is caramelized. Add the flour and stir frequently for about 5 minutes, or until thickened. Add the milk and thyme and blend thoroughly. Stir occasionally over medium heat for about 15 minutes, or until the soup thickens. Add the corn and salt and cook for about 5 minutes longer, or until the corn is tender. Increase the heat to high and add the crabmeat and cream to the soup, stirring frequently for about 5 minutes, or until the mixture is thoroughly heated through and coats the back of the spoon. Remove from the heat and add the pepper and hot pepper sauce. Serve immediately.

MAKES 6 TO 8 SERVINGS

 German Weissbier, Belgian Witbier, or Belgian Lambic

Chardonnay

THE ART OF THE PERFECT
SANDWICH
AND SALAD

SANDWICHES

Grilled Club Sandwich
with Brie and Raspberry
Honey Mayonnaise

Fit for the King Peanut Butter
and Banana Sandwich

Reuben with Chowchow,
Swiss Cheese, and Thousand
Island Dijonnaise

Tupelo Honey Chicken
Sandwich with Havarti Cheese
and Cranberry Mayonnaise

Fried Green Tomato and Grilled
Portobello Sandwich with Basil
Roasted Red Pepper Mayonnaise

Grateful Dead Black Bean
Burger with Cilantro
Lime Mayonnaise

Southern Fried Chicken BLT

SALADS

Pickled Green Tomato Salad
with Fresh Mozzarella

Bacony Egg Salad

Peachy Grilled Chicken Salad
with Pecan Vinaigrette

Spinach Salad with Roasted
Beets, Goat Cheese,
Peppered Bacon, and
Garlic Ranch Dressing

Southern Spring Salad
with Basil Vinaigrette

Tupelo Honey Coleslaw

Get Your Leafy Greens Quota
Salad with Sherry Vinaigrette

Not so long ago, the lowly sandwich was typically a slab of ham, some French's mustard, and two slices of Wonder Bread. The humble salad was a wedge of iceberg and a hothouse tomato drizzled with the Wishbone of your choice. How far we've come! These days, the art of the sandwich and salad is as creative a playing field as any arena for entrée concoctions. Sandwiches are no longer relegated to lunchtime; likewise, the salad is no longer pigeonholed as a humble sidekick. Both have claimed their rightful place at the table, front and center.

At Tupelo Honey Cafe, we approach the sandwich and salad each as blank canvases, begging for imagination and color. We believe two slices of artisanal bread merit only the freshest, finest, and most mouthwatering combination of ingredients. Our salad bowls are filled with nature's palette of greens, grains, and goodness.

Part of our passion stems from our town's great love of the arts and our long history of reverence for the creative spirit. Just sip from Asheville's bountiful galleries filled with paintings, fiber arts, sculpture, jewelry, glass, ceramics, metalwork, and mixed media masterpieces. Wander down to the River Arts District and observe our community of artists at work with wheel, brush, torch, fire, loom, and clay. Absorb our musical mix of Celtic, bluegrass, classical, jazz, singer/songwriter, alternative; our performance artist community of dancers and thespians and street buskers and poets. Experience our bookstores, where writers and readers mingle together to exchange ideas about their craft.

Explore some of the surrounding HandMade in America trails, weaving in and out of mountain coves and valleys, introducing you to the cradle of American craft. Soak in the legacy of innovative art begun in the 1930s at Black Mountain College with its legion of distinguished teachers, thinkers, and students: Merce Cunningham, Willem de Kooning, Buckminster Fuller, John Cage, Robert Rauschenberg, Cy Twombly, and Charles Olson.

We believe our kitchen is a similar incubator for the culinary avant garde Asheville deserves. And our finesse with the sandwich and salad demonstrates our respect for the gift of taking simple ideas and transforming them into something worthy of celebration and accolade.

If a club is your default when it comes to ordering a sandwich, you'll never settle for mediocrity in your club again after you try this. The addition of a creamy Brie raises the bar from club to country club. Use high-quality ingredients—turkey, ham, and freshly baked wheat bread—and, by all means, don't forget the Raspberry Honey Mayonnaise. Sublime.

GRILLED CLUB SANDWICH WITH BRIE AND RASPBERRY HONEY MAYONNAISE

3 ounces thinly sliced baked ham

3 ounces thinly sliced turkey breast

2 ounces Brie cheese, cut into (½-inch) sliced wedges

1 tablespoon unsalted butter, at room temperature

3 slices artisan whole wheat bread

2 tablespoons Raspberry Honey Mayonnaise (page 34)

Romaine lettuce

1 tomato, sliced

In a sauté pan or skillet over medium heat, layer the ham and turkey, overlapping the slices. Heat for 1 minute or until warmed through, then turn over with a spatula. Place the Brie slices on top of the meats and continue heating for 1 minute. Move the meat and cheese to the side of the pan. Lightly butter the bread slices and place butter-side down in the pan, one at a time if necessary, grilling for about 2 minutes, or until golden. Construct your sandwich in this order: 1 slice bread, ham and melted Brie, 1 tablespoon mayonnaise, lettuce, 2 slices tomato, 1 slice bread, turkey with melted Brie, 1 tablespoon mayonnaise, lettuce, 2 slices tomato, and (whew!) the last slice of bread. Cut into quarters, securing each quarter with a toothpick.

MAKES 1 SUBSTANTIAL SERVING

 brown ale

oaked Chardonnay

Tupelo's (Tupelo, Mississippi, that is) favorite son, Elvis, loved peanut butter and banana sandwiches, so we make this one as a tribute to The King. It's a hunk-a-hunk of Tupelo love guaranteed to leave you all shook up.

FIT FOR THE KING PEANUT BUTTER **AND** BANANA SANDWICH

1½ teaspoons unsalted butter, at room temperature

2 tablespoons peanut butter

2 slices Texas toast

½ ripe banana, cut lengthwise into 3 pieces

1 tablespoon tupelo honey

1 to 2 tablespoons mayonnaise

Over low heat, melt the butter in a sauté pan or skillet. Spread the peanut butter on one side of each slice of bread, add banana slices on 1 slice of bread, and drizzle with the honey. Place the bread peanut butter side up in the pan. Spread the mayonnaise on top of the peanut butter side of the second slice of bread. Combine the slices of bread into a sandwich and griddle until both sides are golden brown and the peanut butter begins to melt.

MAKES 1 SANDWICH

Belgian Witbier

Riesling

Black Mountain College

Black Mountain College, located just outside Asheville until its closing in the 1950s, was an incubator for the avant-garde. Founded in 1933 in Black Mountain, North Carolina, this small experimental school produced some of America's more influential twentieth-century artists, poets, designers, and thinkers. Buckminster Fuller designed the first geodesic dome, Merce Cunningham formed his dance company, and John Cage staged his first happening. Teachers included Willem de Kooning and Josef Albers; guest lecturers included Albert Einstein and William Carlos Williams. The site of the school at Lake Eden is now home to the Lake Eden Arts Festival, a celebration of world music and culture.

A Reuben by any other name would taste simply ordinary compared with ours. The difference is the chowchow and taking the time to make your own Thousand Island dressing. Recipes for both follow. Be sure you start with quality rye bread from your local bakery.

REUBEN WITH CHOWCHOW, SWISS CHEESE, AND THOUSAND ISLAND DIJONNAISE

2 tablespoons Dijon mustard

2 tablespoons stone-ground mustard

10 ounces sliced deli corned beef, divided into 4 portions

4 tablespoons chowchow (recipe follows)

4 slices artisanal rye bread

1 tablespoon unsalted butter, at room temperature

4 slices Swiss cheese

4 tablespoons Thousand Island dressing (recipe follows)

Combine the Dijon mustard and the stone-ground mustard in a small bowl and set aside. Place a large sauté pan or skillet over medium heat. Place 1 portion of the corned beef in the hot pan. Layer 2 tablespoons chowchow and then top with a second portion of corned beef. Heat for 4 minutes before flipping the meat over and cooking 3 to 4 minutes longer, until the chowchow is heated through. Move the meat to one side of the pan. Spread the bread slices with butter and place butter side down in the skillet over medium heat until lightly browned. Remove the bread from the pan and place grill side down on a plate, layering cheese on top, grill side up, before adding the corned beef and chowchow combination. Place the additional bread slice on top and cut in half so you can see the layers of cheese, corned beef, and chowchow. Repeat for the second sandwich. Serve with the dressing and the mustard mixture as 2 dipping sauces.

MAKES 2 SERVINGS

Scottish Ale

Garnacha

This zesty concoction clearly makes our Reuben a superstar, but don't be put off by the time and effort it takes to put together. Not only is it worth it for this sandwich, but the chowchow will keep in the refrigerator in a sealed container for two weeks. And it's delicious with roast pork, fried fish, a supper of beans and cornbread, or as a surprise topping for your next burger or barbecue supper.

TRADITIONAL APPALACHIAN CHOWCHOW

4 cups finely chopped green cabbage (about 1 medium head)

1 Roma tomato, diced

2 tablespoons diced roasted red bell pepper

½ cup diced sweet onion (such as Vidalia)

¼ teaspoon hot pepper sauce

1 tablespoon sugar

3 tablespoons cider vinegar

1 teaspoon sea salt

⅛ teaspoon ground turmeric

¼ teaspoon Dijon mustard

½ teaspoon stone-ground mustard

In an 8-cup stainless-steel pot, thoroughly combine all the ingredients and place on high heat until the mixture begins to simmer. Decrease the heat to medium and simmer for about 20 minutes longer, or until the cabbage is translucent. Remove from the heat and allow to cool to room temperature before serving or refrigerating.

MAKES 2 CUPS

THOUSAND ISLAND DRESSING

1 cup mayonnaise

4 tablespoons sweet pickle relish

2 tablespoons plus 1½ teaspoons ketchup

1 teaspoon freshly squeezed lemon juice

1 teaspoon Worcestershire sauce

¼ teaspoon salt

¼ teaspoon freshly ground black pepper

Combine all the ingredients with a wire whisk in a small bowl. Refrigerate the dressing in an airtight container for up to 2 weeks.

MAKES 1½ CUPS

The combination of creamy Havarti, slightly sweet and tart cranberries, and marinated grilled chicken is a real crowd pleaser. This is great anytime but particularly fun when grilling for a get-together and when you want something different from (but equally simple to make as) a cheeseburger.

TUPELO HONEY CHICKEN SANDWICH WITH HAVARTI CHEESE AND CRANBERRY MAYONNAISE

1 (6-ounce) boneless, skinless chicken breast

1 cup Tupelo Honey Chicken Marinade (recipe follows)

1 (2-ounce) slice Havarti cheese

2 teaspoons unsalted butter, at room temperature

2 slices artisanal sourdough bread

Cranberry Mayonnaise (page 34)

Romaine lettuce

Place the chicken in a sealable plastic bag with the marinade and refrigerate overnight. Remove the chicken and discard the marinade. In a large sauté pan or skillet, grill the chicken over medium heat for 4 to 5 minutes per side, until no longer pink and cooked to a temperature of 160°F, placing the cheese on top of the chicken 1 minute before finishing. Move the chicken to the side of the pan. Lightly butter the bread slices and place them butter side down in the pan over medium heat until golden brown. Slather the mayonnaise on both bread slices and layer the lettuce, chicken with Havarti, and the second bread slice to finish the sandwich.

MAKES 1 SERVING

 pale ale

Garnacha

TUPELO HONEY
CHICKEN MARINADE

1½ cups pineapple juice

⅔ cup olive oil

⅔ cup soy sauce

4 cloves garlic, finely chopped

2 tablespoons finely minced fresh ginger (from 4-inch piece ginger)

Combine all the ingredients in a medium bowl using a wire whisk. Refrigerate in an airtight container for 3 to 4 weeks.

MAKES ABOUT 2 CUPS

"These days people worry so much about their hearts that they don't eat heavy. The way folks were meant to eat is the way my family ate when I was growing up . . . We ate till we got *tired.* Then we went 'Whoo!' and leaned back and wholeheartedly expressed how much we regretted that we couldn't summon up the strength, right then, to eat some more."

—Roy Blount Jr., *Long Time Leaving*

This sandwich is guaranteed to tempt even the staunchest omnivore to become vegetarian, just so he can indulge in this explosive combination of flavors on a regular basis. It will remind you of Mediterranean fare, with the earthy portobello teamed with tangy green tomatoes, basil, and roasted red bell peppers.

FRIED GREEN TOMATO AND GRILLED PORTOBELLO SANDWICH WITH BASIL ROASTED RED PEPPER MAYONNAISE

1 cup balsamic vinegar

½ teaspoon dried oregano

1 tablespoon chopped fresh basil

¼ teaspoon sea salt

⅛ teaspoon freshly ground black pepper

1 cup olive oil

2 large portobello mushrooms, stems and gills discarded

2 teaspoons unsalted butter, at room temperature

2 slices artisanal sourdough bread

2 ounces softened goat cheese

Romaine lettuce

3 slices Fried Green Tomatoes (page 178)

2 tablespoons Basil Roasted Red Pepper Mayonnaise (recipe follows)

In a medium bowl, combine the vinegar, oregano, basil, salt, and pepper, whisking to combine. Slowly drizzle in the olive oil, whisking the whole time until the vinaigrette is thoroughly blended. Add the mushrooms to the bowl and toss with the vinaigrette marinade. Cover and let rest for 1 hour at room temperature. Drain the mushrooms. Heat your grill to medium and grill the mushrooms for 2 to 3 minutes on each side, until tender. Lightly butter the bread slices and place butter down in a skillet over medium heat until grilled and lightly browned. Assemble the sandwich by spreading the goat cheese on 1 slice of bread and layering the lettuce, fried green tomatoes, portobellos, mayonnaise, more lettuce, and the remaining bread slice.

MAKES 1 SERVING

 Pilsner

 unoaked Chardonnay

BASIL ROASTED RED PEPPER MAYONNAISE

4 tablespoons mayonnaise

4 large fresh basil leaves, minced

2 tablespoons diced roasted red bell pepper

½ teaspoon freshly squeezed lemon juice

½ teaspoon sea salt

½ teaspoon freshly ground black pepper

In a small bowl, combine all the ingredients, using a fork and a whisklike motion. Refrigerate in an airtight container for up to 2 weeks.

MAKES ¾ CUP

c. 1950

Douglas Ellington

Strolling around downtown Asheville, you'll recognize its reputation as one of the most important American cities for outstanding Art Deco architecture. Architect Douglas Ellington's legacy is notable with his designs for Asheville City Hall, S&W Cafeteria, First Baptist Church of Asheville, and Asheville High School. He eventually had a self-designed summer home in Asheville where he lived until his death in 1960.

Our chef, Brian, followed Jerry and the boys for many years and in the process perfected this bursting-with-flavor black bean burger. Dress it with your favorite hamburger condiments or try this with our Cilantro Lime Mayonnaise. It will have you singing about teddy bears.

GRATEFUL DEAD BLACK BEAN BURGER WITH CILANTRO LIME MAYONNAISE

1 tablespoon olive oil

½ cup peeled, shredded carrots

½ cup corn, frozen, or cut from 1 large ear

½ cup diced roasted red bell pepper

½ cup diced poblano chile

½ cup diced Vidalia onion

½ cup diced celery

1 tablespoon chopped garlic

1 cup firm tofu

2 (15-ounce) cans black beans, drained and rinsed

1 tablespoon minced fresh cilantro

Juice of ½ lime

1½ teaspoons ground cumin

1 tablespoon chili powder

½ teaspoon sea salt

¼ teaspoon freshly ground black pepper

1 teaspoon hot pepper sauce

2 cups panko bread crumbs

2 cups canola oil

8 artisanal hamburger rolls

Cilantro Lime Mayonnaise (recipe follows)

continued on next page

 Belgian Saison

Sangiovese

Heat the olive oil in a sauté pan or skillet over high heat and stir the carrots, corn, bell pepper, poblano, onion, celery, and garlic for about 5 minutes, or until tender. Remove from the heat and cool for 10 minutes. Puree the tofu in a food processor or blender until smooth. Combine the sautéed vegetable mixture with the beans, cilantro, lime juice, cumin, chili powder, salt, pepper, and hot pepper sauce. Working with 2 cups at a time, pulse the bean and vegetable mixture until coarsely chopped and transfer to a large bowl. Add the tofu and bread crumbs and mix by hand until you can form 8 burger patties. Heat the canola oil in a heavy-bottomed pan or skillet on high heat until the oil begins to bubble. Put the bean patties into the hot oil and cook on each side for about 5 minutes, or until the outside is crispy. Serve on an artisanal roll with mayonnaise.

MAKES 8 BURGERS

CILANTRO LIME MAYONNAISE

6 tablespoons mayonnaise

2 tablespoons freshly squeezed lime juice

2 tablespoons minced fresh cilantro

1/8 teaspoon sea salt

1/8 teaspoon freshly ground black pepper

In a small bowl, combine all the ingredients, blending well.

MAKES 2 SERVINGS

Soaking the chicken overnight in buttermilk renders the end chicken juicy and tender beyond belief. This yummy sandwich is at its sublime-ist when local tomatoes are in season and you've got access to incredible bacon, like western North Carolina's Hickory Nut Gap or bacon from Alan "The Bacon King" Benton in east Tennessee. Combining these flavors on a summer night will make you swoon.

SOUTHERN FRIED CHICKEN BLT

2 (6-ounce) boneless, skinless chicken breasts

2 cups buttermilk

4 slices bacon

2 cups canola oil

1 cup all-purpose flour

2 tablespoons cornstarch

¾ teaspoon sea salt

½ teaspoon freshly ground black pepper

2 artisan hoagie rolls

2 teaspoons unsalted butter

4 teaspoons Dijonnaise (recipe follows)

Romaine lettuce

1 red ripe tomato, sliced

Place the chicken in a small nonreactive bowl and cover with the buttermilk. Cover with plastic wrap and refrigerate to marinate overnight or for at least 1 hour. In a cast-iron skillet, cook the bacon until crisp, transferring to paper towels when done. Add the canola oil to the bacon drippings in the skillet and increase the heat to medium or 350°F, until the oil begins to bubble. In a second bowl, combine the flour, cornstarch, salt, and pepper, mixing thoroughly. With kitchen tongs, remove the chicken breasts from the buttermilk and dredge in the dry ingredients mixture until the chicken is completely coated. Carefully place the chicken, using tongs, into the hot oil and brown for about 5 minutes per side, or until the breast is golden brown and crispy. Remove the chicken from the hot oil and drain on paper towels. Slice the rolls in half and lightly butter each side before placing butter side down in a sauté pan or skillet over medium heat until grilled.

Build your sandwich like this: on the bottom roll, put 1 teaspoon dijonnaise, then layer lettuce. Place 1 teaspoon dijonnaise on top of the lettuce and alternate dijonnaise with the remaining ingredients in this order: tomato, chicken, and bacon. Cover with the top half of the hoagie roll. Layering the dijonnaise will help keep this mondo sandwich together.

MAKES 2 SERVINGS

🍺 **extra special bitter ale**

🍷 **Pinot Noir**

This is a fantastic sandwich spread for so many combinations from ham and cheese to roast beef to grilled salmon. It also rocks on a juicy burger.

DIJONNAISE

2 tablespoons mayonnaise

1 teaspoon stone-ground mustard

1 teaspoon Dijon mustard

$\frac{1}{8}$ teaspoon sea salt

$\frac{1}{8}$ teaspoon freshly ground black pepper

Place all the ingredients in a small bowl and whisk until thoroughly combined.

MAKES 2 SERVINGS

Yet another way to enjoy the versatile green tomato, this spicy salad combines sweet with hot, and Asian-influenced flavors reminiscent of an old spice trade route with a hint of someplace South of the Border.

PICKLED GREEN TOMATO SALAD WITH FRESH MOZZARELLA

1 cup cider vinegar

¼ cup firmly packed brown sugar

1 teaspoon sea salt

½ cup water

1 cup olive oil

1 teaspoon minced garlic

2 teaspoons minced fresh ginger

1 teaspoon mustard seed

1 teaspoon freshly ground black pepper

½ teaspoon ground turmeric

½ teaspoon ground cumin

½ teaspoon ground coriander

½ teaspoon curry powder

⅛ teaspoon cayenne pepper

6 green tomatoes, each cut into 8 wedges

½ cup thinly sliced green onion, white and green parts

2 jalapeño peppers, seeded and sliced into thin rings

6 thick slices fresh mozzarella cheese

Sliced red bell pepper, for garnish

Thinly sliced fresh basil, for garnish

In a heavy saucepan, bring the vinegar, brown sugar, salt, and water to a boil and keep warm. In a sauté pan or skillet, heat the olive oil, garlic, ginger, mustard seed, black pepper, turmeric, cumin, coriander, curry powder, and cayenne over medium heat for 2 to 3 minutes, until fragrant. In a large bowl, combine the vinegar and oil mixtures to create a warm pickling liquid. Add the tomatoes, green onion, and jalapeño to the pickling liquid, cover, and let stand at room temperature for at least 4 hours or refrigerate overnight. To serve, arrange the cheese slices on a platter. Drain the tomato wedges and place them on top of the cheese. Garnish with the bell pepper and basil.

MAKES 6 SERVINGS

dark lager

Pinot Noir

The marriage of bacon and egg is a match made in heaven, and this salad is delicious stuffed into a fresh hollowed tomato, eaten as a satisfying sandwich on hearty bread, or munched with chips or crostini as an appetizer or snack. Peppered bacon is what sets this apart from your run-of-the-mill egg salad.

BACONY EGG SALAD

8 eggs

6 strips peppered bacon, cooked until crispy

5 tablespoons mayonnaise

1 teaspoon mustard powder

¼ teaspoon freshly ground black pepper

⅛ teaspoon sea salt

Place the eggs in a heavy saucepan and cover them with cold water. Bring to a boil over high heat, cooking for 12 minutes. Remove the eggs from the heat, drain, and cover with ice and cold water. When the eggs have cooled, peel and chop; place the chopped eggs in a bowl. Crumble the bacon into pieces and add to the eggs. Blend the mixture together with the mayonnaise, mustard powder, pepper, and salt.

MAKES 4 SERVINGS

Belgian Witbier

French Chardonnay (white Burgundy)

When we eat this salad, we pay homage to one of our region's defining landmarks. Drive just south of Asheville to Gaffney, South Carolina, and you'll see an enormous water tower in the shape of a peach. It's something of a shrine to those of us who long for peach season each summer. You can mix up a batch of our peach salsa with frozen peaches if fresh are not available.

PEACHY GRILLED CHICKEN SALAD WITH PECAN VINAIGRETTE

1 (6-ounce) boneless, skinless chicken breast

1 cup Tupelo Honey Chicken Marinade (page 77)

Seasonal fresh salad greens

½ cup Peach Fennel Salsa (page 5)

Pecan Vinaigrette (page 31)

Marinate the chicken breast in the marinade in a sealable plastic bag or covered container overnight in the refrigerator. Remove the chicken, discarding the marinade, and grill or cook in a cast-iron skillet over high heat for 3 to 4 minutes on each side, until the chicken is tender and no longer pink in the middle. Transfer the chicken to a cutting board and slice thinly. Place the salad greens on a plate, top with the chicken slices, and salsa. Serve with the vinaigrette.

MAKES 1 SERVING

 British bitter, American amber ale

Chardonnay, Rioja, Pinot Noir

Roasting fresh beets brings out the natural sweetness of this nutritious root vegetable and balances deliciously with the creamy tang of goat cheese and the saltiness of the bacon. Spinach anchors the entire salad with a bass note of green, leafy goodness. The colors of this salad are an additional selling point. Popeye would be pleased.

SPINACH SALAD WITH ROASTED BEETS, GOAT CHEESE, PEPPERED BACON, AND GARLIC RANCH DRESSING

1 large beet, trimmed and washed

8 ounces fresh spinach

4 slices cooked and crumbled peppered bacon

3 ounces goat cheese

Garlic Ranch Dressing (page 29)

12 grape tomatoes, for garnish

Wrap the beet in foil and bake in a 350°F oven for about 1 hour, or until tender when a knife is inserted. When cool enough to handle, remove the foil and peel and dice the beet. Divide the spinach between 2 plates and top with the beet and bacon. Crumble the goat cheese on top and drizzle with the dressing. Garnish with the grape tomatoes and serve.

MAKES 2 SERVINGS

German Weissbier, Belgian Witbier

French Chardonnay (white Burgundy), American Pinot Noir

This is our house salad at the restaurant and much loved by our regular patrons. No wonder, since it's packed with a delicious combination of nuts, earthy mushrooms, dried berries, and sharp gorgonzola. When our lettuces come in at Sunshot Farm and at other area farms, this is one of the best things on our menu.

SOUTHERN SPRING SALAD
WITH BASIL VINAIGRETTE

4 tablespoons sliced almonds

Spring salad greens mix

4 cremini mushrooms, sliced

2 ounces gorgonzola cheese, crumbled

2 tablespoons dried cranberries

6 grape tomatoes

Basil Vinaigrette (page 27)

Place 2 tablespoons of the almonds on a rimmed sheet pan and bake in a 375°F oven for about 8 minutes, or until golden. Arrange the salad greens on a plate. Top with the mushrooms, gorgonzola, the remaining 2 tablespoons almonds, the cranberries, and grape tomatoes. Serve with the vinaigrette.

MAKES 1 SERVING

 Scottish ale

Carménerè

Lexington Ave. curb market c. 1940

From barbecues to fish frys, coleslaw is the preferred side. Cooks around the South will swear by theirs, whether it's hot and vinegary or creamy and slightly sweet. Your choice depends on your mood, but we think ours, which is a mash-up of creamy and vinegary, is pretty darn good anytime. And it's pretty to look at to boot.

TUPELO HONEY COLESLAW

4 cups shredded green cabbage (from 1 medium cabbage)

2 cups shredded red cabbage (from 1 small red cabbage)

1 cup peeled, shredded carrot (about 2 large carrots)

2 tablespoons red wine vinegar

4½ teaspoons ketchup

5 tablespoons sugar

1 cup mayonnaise

2 tablespoons Dijon mustard

2 tablespoons stone-ground mustard

⅛ teaspoon hot pepper sauce

4½ teaspoons Worcestershire Sauce

½ teaspoon sea salt

¼ teaspoon freshly ground black pepper

1 cup canola oil

Combine the green cabbage, red cabbage, and carrot in a large bowl. In a separate bowl, combine the vinegar, ketchup, and sugar and stir until the sugar is dissolved. Put the vinegar mixture in a food processor and add the mayonnaise, Dijon mustard, stone-ground mustard, hot pepper sauce, Worcestershire, salt, and pepper. Blend and slowly drizzle in the canola oil until the mixture is emulsified. Combine the vegetables with the dressing, adding the dressing a little at a time until it suits your personal slaw to dressing ratio. Any leftover dressing can be refrigerated in an airtight container for 1 week.

MAKES 4 TO 6 SERVINGS

We're all told to eat them, aren't we? This salad is a great way to maximize the nutritional values of these fabulous vegetables by consuming them raw but not unadorned. The addition of beets, grape tomatoes, and shredded carrots adds a splash of color, as well as extra blasts of vitamins A and C. This is a great autumn and winter salad.

GET YOUR LEAFY GREENS QUOTA SALAD WITH SHERRY VINAIGRETTE

½ medium beet

1 teaspoon olive oil

4 tablespoons toasted
   sunflower seeds

⅛ teaspoon sea salt

⅛ teaspoon freshly ground
   black pepper

2 cups chopped leafy green
   vegetables (such as Swiss
   chard, kale, bok choy, and
   napa cabbage)

2 tablespoons peeled, shredded
   carrots

6 grape tomatoes

2 ounces goat cheese

Sherry Vinaigrette (recipe
   follows)

Preheat the oven to 350°F and wrap the beet in aluminum foil. Bake for about 1 hour, or until tender when pierced with a knife. Remove and cool before peeling and dicing. Heat the olive oil in a sauté pan or skillet and sauté the sunflower seeds, salt, and pepper over low heat for 5 to 7 minutes, until lightly toasted. Combine the greens, beet, sunflower seeds, carrots, tomatoes, and goat cheese. Serve with the vinaigrette.

MAKES 1 LARGE DINNER SALAD

Hefeweizen

Sauvignon Blanc

SHERRY VINAIGRETTE

1 shallot, minced

2 cloves garlic, minced

2 teaspoons minced fresh
parsley

1 teaspoon minced fresh
thyme leaves

½ teaspoon Dijon mustard

½ teaspoon stone-ground
mustard

½ teaspoon sea salt

¼ teaspoon freshly ground
black pepper

½ cup sherry vinegar

1 cup olive oil

In a food processor, combine the shallot, garlic, parsley, thyme, Dijon mustard, stone-ground mustard, salt, and pepper. Puree the ingredients for 1 minute. With the processor running, add the vinegar and then slowly drizzle in the olive oil until the dressing emulsifies.

MAKES ABOUT 1½ CUPS

FISH OUT OF WATER

Shrimp and Goat Cheese Grits with
Roasted Red Pepper Sauce

Chorizo-Baked Sea Scallops with Basil Cream Sauce

Spice-Crusted Tuna with Seared Crab
Cakes and Lemon Hollandaise

Blackened Catfish with Sunshot Salsa

Char-Grilled Swordfish with Marinated
Green Tomatoes and Rosemary Aioli

Almond-Crusted Trout with Blackened
Crawfish and Roasted Red Pepper Butter

Pecan-Crusted Red Snapper with Spiced
Black Beans and Orange Cilantro Butter

Curry-Spiced Halibut with Chard and Oven-
Roasted Tomatoes in Lemon Beurre Blanc

Buttery Cracker-Baked Oysters with Rémoulade

Bronzed Wild Sockeye Salmon
with Roasted Corn Salsa

Smoked Salmon–Wrapped Sea Scallops
with Capers and Pickled Onion Aioli

Asheville is like a big, colorful, lively aquarium brimming with every possible personality imaginable. And like an aquarium, Asheville welcomes all kinds of fish. When you are here, you may find several schools you'd like to swim with, or you may feel drawn to one special type. Whatever you decide, looking around, you'll see thousands of different manifestations of our species, all swimming happily in the same water.

But as harmonious as we strive to be in Asheville, make no mistake that individuality and self-expression are a way of life. In other words, there's no need to worry about fitting the proverbial square peg in the proverbial round hole because we have every manner of holes and pegs all right here. Whatever shape you are, you're going to fit in.

Just look at our roster of past residents: Frederick Law Olmsted, visionary father of landscape architecture in America, left his mark not only on Asheville at Biltmore but inspired our country to safeguard its green spaces and national parks. There's the late Bob Moog, a trailblazer in the field of music electronics, inventor of the music synthesizer, and producer of Theremins. Legend has it George Gershwin penned "Rhapsody in Blue" while in Asheville. Walt Disney once worked here as a draftsman. Spanish architect Rafael Guastavino, whose famous vaulted tile arches and domes adorn many New York landmarks, retired here and created the beautiful St. Lawrence Basilica. Writers Thomas Wolfe and O. Henry are both permanent residents at Riverside Cemetery.

It stands to reason, then, that at Tupelo Honey, we look at every fish as a great idea just waiting to be born. We try to let each catch speak for itself through its freshness as well as the complementary flavors we contribute. Sometimes, we let the taste of genius arrive plated and unadulterated. However you like your fish, we believe these recipes are all individual standouts.

"When my mind's unsettled,
When I don't feel spruce,
When my nerves get frazzled,
When my flesh gets loose—
What knits
Me back together's grits.
Grits with gravy, grits with cheese.
Grits with bacon, Grits with peas . . .
Grits, grits, it's grits I sing
Grits fits in with anything."

—Roy Blount Jr., *One Fell Soup*

Shrimp and grits is iconic fare in the Carolina Low Country, where it's been a favorite on-the-boat breakfast for shrimpers for years. The dish was famously brought to the nation's attention when *New York Times* legendary food writer Craig Claiborne, a Mississippi native, had dinner with Chef Bill Neal at Crook's Corner in Chapel Hill, North Carolina. With that prescient and sacred heritage right in our backyard, we take our shrimp and grits very, very seriously. The goat cheese grits is Tupelo Honey's own signature twist.

SHRIMP AND GOAT CHEESE GRITS WITH ROASTED RED PEPPER SAUCE

2 tablespoons plus
   1½ teaspoons olive oil

1 pound large uncooked shrimp,
   peeled, deveined, and tails
   removed

1 tablespoon minced garlic

½ cup thinly sliced roasted red
   bell pepper

2 tablespoons Creole Spice
   (recipe follows)

¼ cup dry white wine (such as
   Sauvignon Blanc)

3 tablespoons unsalted cold
   butter

Goat Cheese Basil Grits
   (page 179)

Heat the olive oil in a large skillet on high heat. Add the shrimp and garlic and cook for about 4 minutes, or until the shrimp begins to turn a little pink. Add the bell peppers and Creole spice and cook for about 2 minutes, or until the peppers are heated through. Add the wine and cook for 1 to 2 minutes, just until the shrimp turns pink. Remove from the heat and add the butter, swirling the pan to combine all the liquids. Serve the shrimp over the grits and top with the warm sauce left in the skillet.

MAKES 4 SERVINGS

 Belgian Witbier

old vine Zinfandel, Gewurztraminer

CREOLE SPICE

1 tablespoon sugar

2½ teaspoons sea salt

1 tablespoon smoked paprika

2 teaspoons cayenne pepper

1 teaspoon freshly ground black
   pepper

1 teaspoon white pepper

Combine the ingredients and enjoy!

MAKES ¼ CUP

View from across Pack Square c. 1910

The saltiness of the chorizo paired with the sweetness of plump sea scallops creates a beautiful juxtaposition. This is a rich dish, one where you push back from the table and say "Whoo!" to paraphrase Roy Blount Jr. Look for scallops that are creamy color or a little pink and ask for dry-packed.

CHORIZO-BAKED SEA SCALLOPS WITH BASIL CREAM SAUCE

1 cup fresh chorizo, removed from casing (2 sausages)

2 tablespoons unsalted butter

1 cup panko bread crumbs

2 tablespoons grated fresh Parmesan cheese

¼ large Vidalia onion, thinly sliced

1 tablespoon canola oil

16 fresh jumbo sea scallops

2 teaspoons minced garlic

2 tablespoons thinly sliced roasted red bell pepper

2 tablespoons minced fresh basil

⅓ cup dry white wine (such as Sauvignon Blanc)

½ cup heavy cream

½ teaspoon freshly ground black pepper

Sauté the chorizo over medium heat in a heavy dry medium sauté pan or skillet for 4 to 5 minutes, or until cooked through and completely browned. Drain the excess oil and put the chorizo into a small bowl. Melt the butter in the pan. In a medium bowl, combine the bread crumbs, melted butter, chorizo, and cheese, mixing well. Set aside.

Preheat the oven's broiler. In the pan, heat the onion over low heat until caramelized, stirring often, and set aside. Heat the canola oil in a medium sauté pan or skillet over high heat and allow the oil to just begin to bubble. Add the scallops and cook for about 2 minutes, or until golden brown. Turn the scallops and cook for about 2 minutes longer, or until the scallops are golden brown on both sides. Add the garlic, bell pepper, caramelized onion, basil, and white wine and cook for about 2 minutes, or until the flavors are thoroughly combined. Add the cream and pepper and cook for about 3 minutes longer, or until the scallops are cooked through and firm to the touch. Place the scallop mixture in an ovenproof shallow casserole dish. Finish by sprinkling the chorizo panko mixture over the scallops and placing them under the broiler for 2 to 4 minutes, until browned.

MAKES 2 SERVINGS

🍺 Irish stout

🍷 Malbec

Just about everybody has their favorite style of crab cake from Maryland to New England to New Orleans. We make ours from scratch and pair them with zesty blackened tuna and a sunny hollandaise. For a fantastic brunch, serve the crab cakes with a poached egg on top. Spoon over the warm, lemony hollandaise and shout hallelujah!

SPICE-CRUSTED TUNA WITH SEARED CRAB CAKES AND LEMON HOLLANDAISE

4 sashimi-grade 6-ounce tuna steaks

1 cup Blackening Spice (page 141)

½ cup canola oil

Seared Crab Cakes (recipe follows)

Lemon Hollandaise Sauce (recipe follows)

Dredge the tuna in the blackening spice until well coated. Heat the canola oil in a large sauté pan or skillet over high heat. Place the tuna in the hot oil and cook for 2 to 3 minutes on each side, until the tuna is medium rare and still red in the middle.

To assemble the dish, place a tuna steak and a crab cake on each plate and pour the warm hollandaise sauce on top. Serve immediately.

MAKES 4 SERVINGS

Grove Park Inn

Built from the fortune made by E. W. Grove's famous curative Tasteless Chill Tonic, the Grove Park Inn was opened in 1913, and has cared for an impressive roster of famous guests—Thomas Edison, F. Scott Fitzgerald, and George Gershwin among them. This massive and imposing stone structure overlooks the city of Asheville and adjoins a golf course by the famed designer Donald Ross.

 English bitter ale

Pinot Noir

SEARED CRAB CAKES

CRAB CAKE SEASONING MIXTURE

1 teaspoon canola oil

⅓ cup finely diced Vidalia onion

⅓ cup diced celery

⅓ cup diced roasted red bell pepper

1 teaspoon minced garlic

Juice of ½ lemon

2 teaspoons Worcestershire Sauce

2 teaspoons hot pepper sauce

½ teaspoon fresh thyme leaves

½ teaspoon sea salt

½ teaspoon freshly ground black pepper

1 bay leaf

4 teaspoons sherry

1 egg white

3 tablespoons mayonnaise

1 pound lump crabmeat

½ cup panko bread crumbs

1 tablespoon canola oil

1 tablespoon unsalted butter

To prepare the crab cake seasoning mixture, heat the canola oil in a sauté pan or skillet over high heat. Sauté the onion, celery, and bell pepper for about 3 minutes, or until the vegetables are just tender. Lower the heat to medium and add the garlic, lemon juice, Worcestershire, hot pepper sauce, thyme, salt, pepper, bay leaf, and sherry. Simmer for about 15 minutes, or until most of the liquid has evaporated. Drain any excess liquid and remove the bay leaf. Reserve ½ cup of the seasoning mixture and save the rest for another use, such as chicken salad or tuna salad. Kept covered in the refrigerator, the seasoning mixture will keep for up to 30 days.

In a medium bowl, whisk the egg white until frothy and it begins to stiffen. Gently fold in the mayonnaise and the reserved seasoning mixture with a rubber spatula. Add the crabmeat and bread crumbs, combining well, and refrigerate for 1 hour. Combine the canola oil and butter in a large sauté pan or skillet over high heat. Form the crabmeat mixture into 4 patties and place them in the hot oil, cooking them for about 3 minutes on each side, or until golden brown. Keep warm until ready to use.

MAKES 4 SERVINGS

LEMON HOLLANDAISE SAUCE

3 egg yolks

¼ teaspoon sea salt

⅛ teaspoon hot pepper sauce

2 tablespoons freshly squeezed
   lemon juice

2 tablespoons water

2 tablespoons white wine

8 tablespoons unsalted butter,
   melted

Fill the bottom of a double boiler with water and place over high heat. When the water boils, fit the top pan over the bottom of the double boiler and reduce the heat to low. In a small bowl, whisk together the egg yolks, salt, hot pepper sauce, lemon juice, water, and wine. Pour the egg mixture into the double boiler, whisking constantly for 4 to 5 minutes, until the mixture is light yellow and creamy. Slowly whisk the melted butter into the egg mixture until the sauce coats the back of a spoon. Turn off the heat but leave the top pan over the hot water, stirring occasionally, until ready to use.

Above: The Biltmore House, right: George Vanderbilt

Biltmore

Asheville is definitely unique. Case in point—just south of downtown is a 250-room, 175,000-square-foot French château. George Vanderbilt's estate, completed in 1895, includes America's largest home, Biltmore House, designed by architect Richard Morris Hunt. Still privately owned by Vanderbilt's descendents, the estate also includes 8,000 acres of gardens (designed by Frederick Law Olmsted), farm, and forest as well as a winery and a hotel. Biltmore welcomes over a million visitors each year and perpetuates the community's century-old reputation as a mountain playground.

Catfish is often misunderstood and sadly maligned (by the uninitiated) as a bottom-feeding fish. But we're on a catfish campaign to raise awareness for this tasty and affordable fish choice. We use farm-raised fresh catfish that is light and delicious. It marries well with the juicy tomatoes and fresh cilantro in our fresh Sunshot Salsa.

BLACKENED CATFISH
WITH SUNSHOT SALSA

2 tablespoons canola oil

4 (8-ounce) boneless catfish fillets

4 tablespoons Blackening Spice (page 141)

2 cups Sunshot Salsa (page 8)

Cover the bottom of a cast-iron skillet with the canola oil and place over high heat. Dredge the catfish fillets in the blackening spice until thoroughly coated. Cook the fish in the hot oil for 4 to 5 minutes on each side, until the fish is a rich, blackened red color. Serve with generous amounts of the salsa.

MAKES 4 SERVINGS

 pale ale

Sauvignon Blanc

When you see fresh swordfish at your favorite fish mongering spot, don't let it get away. It's a meaty fish and pairs well with this combination of flavors. Try this fantastic blend of green tomato tartness, aromatic rosemary mayonnaise, and char-grilled fish. The aioli is also magnificent on sandwiches or as an accompaniment to grilled chicken.

CHAR-GRILLED SWORDFISH WITH MARINATED GREEN TOMATOES AND ROSEMARY AIOLI

4 (8-ounce) swordfish steaks

1 tablespoon canola oil

½ teaspoon sea salt

½ teaspoon freshly ground black pepper

Marinated Green Tomatoes (recipe follows)

Rosemary Aioli (recipe follows)

Start your grill and bring it to a high heat. Rub the swordfish with the canola oil and season with the salt and pepper. Place the fish on the grill and cook for about 4 minutes on each side, or until the fish is cooked through. Plate the fish and top with the tomatoes and a dollop of aioli before serving.

MAKES 4 SERVINGS

Belgian Tripel, American pale ale

Chardonnay

MARINATED GREEN TOMATOES

1 large green tomato, diced

½ cup sherry vinegar

1 tablespoon balsamic vinegar

½ cup olive oil

¼ teaspoon sea salt

¼ teaspoon freshly ground
   black pepper

1 tablespoon thinly sliced fresh
   basil

Combine all the ingredients in a small bowl and refrigerate for at least 1 hour.

ROSEMARY AIOLI

3 tablespoons mayonnaise

1 tablespoon minced fresh
   rosemary

½ teaspoon roasted garlic
   puree (page 5)

Juice of ½ lemon

¼ teaspoon sea salt

¼ teaspoon freshly ground
   black pepper

Combine all the ingredients in a small bowl until well blended. Refrigerate until ready to serve.

We are blessed in the Blue Ridge to have access to wonderful fresh trout from several local trout farms, including the wonderful Sunburst Trout Farm, right down the road. So, we don't have to put on waders to pull off this amazing entrée. If you happen to be a fisherman (and if you are, our mountains are a great spot to allure and hook), this is a wonderful way to show off your catch. The red pepper butter is heavenly and also goes well with chicken and pork and as a spread for sandwiches.

ALMOND-CRUSTED TROUT WITH BLACKENED CRAWFISH AND ROASTED RED PEPPER BUTTER

ROASTED RED PEPPER BUTTER

4 tablespoons unsalted butter, at room temperature

2 tablespoons diced roasted red bell pepper

½ teaspoon sea salt

½ teaspoon freshly ground black pepper

Juice of ½ lemon

¼ teaspoon roasted garlic puree (page 5)

1 cup blanched almonds

1 cup panko bread crumbs

4 (8-ounce) boneless trout fillets

¼ cup canola oil

8 ounces crawfish tail meat

2 tablespoons Blackening Spice (page 141)

🍺 Belgian Lambic

🍷 oaked Chardonnay

In a food processor or mixer, combine the butter with the bell pepper, ¼ teaspoon of the salt, ¼ teaspoon of the pepper, the lemon juice, and garlic puree. Transfer the butter mixture to a bowl, cover, and refrigerate until ready to prepare the crawfish.

Combine the almonds, bread crumbs, and the remaining ¼ teaspoon salt and ¼ teaspoon pepper in a food processor and blend until fine. Dredge the trout in the almond mixture. Heat the canola oil in a heavy sauté pan or skillet over high heat. Put the trout in the hot oil and cook for about 3 minutes on each side, or until golden brown or the flesh is flaky.

Melt the roasted red pepper butter in a separate sauté pan or skillet and melt over medium-high heat. Coat the crawfish in the blackening spice and place in the melted butter, cooking the meat for 3 to 4 minutes, until heated through. Place each trout fillet on a plate and top with one-quarter of the crawfish and one-quarter of the melted roasted red pepper butter.

MAKES 4 SERVINGS

Fix yourself a drink with a little umbrella on top, and you'll swear you are some place in the islands with this fragrant, flavorful snapper. The dish speaks of Caribbean climes, where many of our Southern foods began their way to our neck of the woods, thanks to the rich culinary legacy of African foodways in the islands.

PECAN-CRUSTED RED SNAPPER WITH SPICED BLACK BEANS AND ORANGE CILANTRO BUTTER

1 cup panko bread crumbs

1 cup pecans

2 tablespoons light brown sugar

1 teaspoon sea salt

1 teaspoon freshly ground black pepper

¼ cup canola oil

4 (8-ounce) boneless snapper fillets, skin removed

1 cup buttermilk

Orange Cilantro Butter (recipe follows)

Spiced Black Beans (recipe follows)

Combine the bread crumbs, pecans, brown sugar, salt, and pepper in a food processor and blend until fine. Transfer to a medium bowl. Preheat the oven to 400°F. Heat the canola oil in a large sauté pan or skillet over medium heat. Dip the snapper in the buttermilk and then dredge in the pecan mixture until thoroughly coated. Cook the fish for 1 minute on each side. Remove from the pan and transfer to an ovenproof baking dish. Bake the fish for 4 to 5 minutes, until cooked through. Top each hot fillet with orange cilantro butter and serve immediately with spiced black beans.

MAKES 4 SERVINGS

Dark lager

Pinot Noir

ORANGE CILANTRO BUTTER

4 tablespoons unsalted butter

1 tablespoon minced cilantro

1 tablespoon orange marmalade

In a mixer or food processor, blend all the ingredients until whipped.

SPICED BLACK BEANS

1 (15-ounce) can black beans with liquid

2 tablespoons balsamic vinegar

Juice of ½ lime

1 tablespoon seeded, minced jalapeño pepper

½ teaspoon ground cumin

¼ teaspoon ground coriander

½ teaspoon salt

½ teaspoon freshly ground black pepper

Combine all the ingredients in a heavy-bottomed pan. Bring to a boil and then reduce the heat to low, simmering for about 20 minutes, or until the liquid is reduced by one-fourth. Add up to ¼ cup water if the beans become too thick.

Shoo Mercy, you say, this sounds too complicated for me! But stand firm. This dish is easy, impressive, and good for you. Light, sweet halibut is the perfect foil to the mineral-richness of the chard and tomatoes, and the lemon beurre blanc complements the whole concoction with a kiss of buttery citrus sunshine. Pair with a Belgian gueuze lambic or a glass of unoaked Chardonnay.

CURRY-SPICED HALIBUT WITH CHARD AND OVEN-ROASTED TOMATOES IN LEMON BEURRE BLANC

SPICE CRUST

2 cups panko bread crumbs

2 teaspoons ground turmeric

2 teaspoons curry powder

2 teaspoons ground cumin

1 teaspoon ground coriander

1 teaspoon sea salt

1 teaspoon freshly ground
   black pepper

1 egg

½ cup whole milk

4 (6-ounce) skinned and boned
   halibut fillets

½ cup canola oil

1 tablespoon olive oil

6 cups Swiss chard, thinly
   sliced

2 cups Oven-Roasted Tomatoes
   (page 48)

1 cup dry white wine

⅛ teaspoon sea salt

⅛ teaspoon freshly ground
   black pepper

2 tablespoons unsalted butter

To make the spice crust, mix all the ingredients in a medium bowl and set aside. Preheat the oven to 400°F. Whisk the egg and milk together in a medium bowl. Place the halibut fillets in a large dish and cover with the egg and milk mixture. Dredge the halibut in the spice crust mixture until completely covered.

Heat the canola oil in a nonstick skillet over high heat until just bubbling. Add the fish and cook for about 3 minutes on each side, or until browned, being careful not to burn. Transfer the fish to a baking pan and bake for about 5 minutes, or until heated through and firm to the touch. Wipe out the excess crumbs from the skillet and add the olive oil, returning to high heat. Add the chard and tomatoes and cook for 1 to 2 minutes, until the chard is just tender. Add the wine, salt, and pepper and cook for about 2 minutes longer, or until the liquid is reduced by one-fourth. Remove the pan from the heat and add the butter, swirling the pan to make the beurre blanc by melting the butter and blending with the wine mixture. Place each fillet on a plate and spoon the vegetable and beurre blanc mixture on top.

MAKES 4 SERVINGS

 German Weissbier, Belgian Witbier

Chardonnay

Oysters come to our restaurant from both the Carolina coast and the Gulf coast, so we have no end of these sweet mollusks during oyster season. The taste of a succulent, fresh oyster is so delicious to begin with, but we like combining its briny plumpness with creamy butter and cheese and a show of spinach for its contrasting vegetal flavor. This is a terrific dish for a holiday table.

BUTTERY CRACKER-BAKED OYSTERS WITH RÉMOULADE

1 teaspoon unsalted butter

9 ounces fresh spinach, chopped

⅓ cup heavy cream

1 tablespoon plus 8 teaspoons freshly grated Parmesan cheese

¼ teaspoon sea salt

½ teaspoon freshly ground black pepper

½ pound fresh, extra-select oysters

½ cup finely ground Ritz Crackers

4 tablespoons unsalted butter, melted

Preheat the oven to 450°F. Butter 4 (8-ounce) ramekins or ovenproof dishes. In a saucepan, combine the butter and spinach and cook over high heat for 2 to 3 minutes, until the spinach is wilted. Add the cream, 1 tablespoon cheese, salt, and pepper and cook over medium heat for about 5 minutes, or until the cheese is melted and combined and the mixture coats the back of a spoon. Divide the creamed spinach mixture into the prepared ramekins and set aside. Dredge the oysters in the crackers until well coated. Place at least 2 oysters on top of each ramekin. Drizzle 1 tablespoon melted butter and sprinkle 2 teaspoons cheese over each ramekin. Bake for 5 to 6 minutes, until barely bubbling, and then place under the broiler for 1 to 2 minutes longer, until the oysters are golden and crisp.

MAKES 4 SERVINGS

 Irish stout

 Petite Syrah

Salmon is touted for its omega-3 fatty acid richness, and that's certainly a great reason to consume it. But we believe dousing it with a touch of bayou flavor and accompanying it with our roasted corn salsa is reason enough. You'll also appreciate the colors of this dish on your plate. It's a beauty.

BRONZED WILD SOCKEYE SALMON WITH ROASTED CORN SALSA

2 tablespoons canola oil

4 (8-ounce) boneless wild sockeye salmon fillets, skin removed

2 tablespoons Creole Spice (page 102)

2 cups Roasted Corn Salsa (page 6)

Heat the canola oil in a heavy sauté pan or skillet over high heat. Pat the salmon fillets with the Creole spice and cook in the hot oil for about 3 minutes on each side, or until cooked through. Serve with generous doses of the salsa.

MAKES 4 SERVINGS

 Belgian Saison

Sauvignon Blanc

Salty and sweet, these scallops are an inventive entrée, but they could also be served as an appetizer or hors d'oeuvre along with some champagne or sparkling wine. Be sure your sea scallops are plump, juicy, and fresh. If you're serving these as an entrée, pair them with our Benne-Coated Asparagus (page 167).

SMOKED SALMON–WRAPPED SEA SCALLOPS WITH CAPERS AND PICKLED ONION AIOLI

4 ounces smoked salmon

16 large sea scallops

1 tablespoon canola oil

1 tablespoon unsalted butter

¼ teaspoon sea salt

¼ teaspoon freshly ground
   black pepper

Pickled Onion Aioli
   (recipe follows)

Slice the salmon lengthwise into strips approximately 1 inch wide, creating 16 slices. Wrap the salmon strips around the circumference of each scallop and secure with a toothpick. Heat the canola oil and butter in a sauté pan or skillet over medium heat. Place the scallops in the pan, flesh side down, and season with the salt and pepper. Cook for about 4 minutes on each side, or until the scallops are hot in the center. Arrange 4 scallops on each serving plate, with 1½ tablespoons aioli.

MAKES 4 TO 6 SERVINGS

PICKLED ONION AIOLI

4 tablespoons mayonnaise

1 tablespoon capers

1 tablespoon Pickled Sweet
   Onions, chopped (page 41)

Juice of ½ lemon

¼ teaspoon sea salt

¼ teaspoon freshly ground
   black pepper

Combine all the ingredients in a small mixing bowl and refrigerate until ready to use.

Irish stout

Pinot Noir

CHICKEN SEVEN WAYS, OR WE STILL LAY

Southern Fried Chicken Breasts
with Cremini Sweet Onion Gravy

Nutty Fried Chicken with Smashed
Sweet Potatoes and Milk Gravy

Southern Chicken Saltimbocca with Country
Ham in a Mushroom Marsala Sauce

Chicken Apple Meat Loaf
with Tarragon Tomato Gravy

Chicken Andouille Stir-Fry
with Orange Jalapeño Glaze

Herb-Roasted Whole Chicken
with Savory Pan Gravy

Blackened Chicken Potpie

Fowl can be foul if it's not honored for the protein rich, succulent meat that it is. Poultry raised freely, without antibiotics and hormones, tastes completely different from processed, mass-produced birds. Respecting the chicken is something near and dear to our hearts in Asheville, where city dwellers raising their own poultry at home protested the effort by community leaders to clip their wings with ordinances prohibiting the keeping of birds within the city limits. They launched a *We Still Lay* campaign in the community and cemented their basic right to bear wings, enjoying fresh eggs in the process.

Truth is, our community paid attention to where our food comes from long before *The Omnivore's Dilemma*. Mountain farms have dotted the Blue Ridge since time immemorial, carried forward by the Cherokee to the early settlers to today's generation of enthusiastic area farmers. In recent years, the Appalachian Sustainable Agriculture Project, a nonprofit organization serving as advocate and network for farmers and foodies, has instigated tailgate markets, published farm directories so chefs know where to shop, and established school-based programs geared toward nurturing a new generation of knowledgeable consumers.

So it is with reverence that we approach the bird at Tupelo Honey. We bathe it in savory gravies, marry it with tart apples or spice, bread it with nutty coating, and submerge it in holy hot cooking oil until it is bronze, crisp, and delicious enough to take its place on the plate alongside mashed sweet potatoes. Once stereotypically banished as rubbery, overcooked hotel meeting fare, the chicken is elevated at Tupelo Honey to its rightful place of honor.

Since there's nothing ordinary about our chicken recipes, indulge in one of these the next time company comes. Your guests will feel eminently distinguished, like rare birds indeed.

"The North seldom tries to fry chicken and this is well; the art cannot be learned north of the Line of Mason and Dixon."

—Mark Twain

Once reserved for the Sunday after-church dinner table, fried chicken is simply too good to hold out for the preacher. In Tupelo Honey vernacular, fried chicken is considered one of the major food groups. The cremini gravy adds just the right touch of gentility and sophistication.

SOUTHERN FRIED CHICKEN BREASTS WITH CREMINI SWEET ONION GRAVY

4 (6-ounce) boneless, skinless chicken breasts

2 cups buttermilk

2 cups canola oil

2 cups all-purpose flour

3 tablespoons cornstarch

1½ teaspoons sea salt

1 teaspoon freshly ground black pepper

Cremini Sweet Onion Gravy (page 13)

Marinate the chicken in the buttermilk overnight in the refrigerator. Place the canola oil in a cast-iron skillet over medium heat to 325°F or until the oil is bubbling. Combine the flour, cornstarch, salt, and pepper in a large bowl. Drain the chicken and discard the buttermilk. Dredge the chicken in the flour mixture until well coated. Fry the chicken in hot oil for 4 to 5 minutes per side, until golden brown. On each plate, ladle some gravy and place a chicken breast on top.

MAKES 4 SERVINGS

 extra special bitter

Sauvignon Blanc

The combination of this nutty dusting for frying the chicken and the sweet and creamy potatoes awash in milk gravy leaves The Colonel in the dust. The roasted mixed nuts add a touch of unexpected complexity. And if you're looking for a family night comfort food fix, this is it.

NUTTY FRIED CHICKEN WITH SMASHED SWEET POTATOES AND MILK GRAVY

6 (6-ounce) boneless, skinless chicken breasts

2 cups buttermilk

2 cups panko bread crumbs

2 cups roasted and salted mixed nuts

2 cups canola oil

Smashed Sweet Potatoes (recipe follows)

Milk Gravy (page 10)

Marinate the chicken in the buttermilk in the refrigerator for at least 1 hour. Combine the bread crumbs and nuts in a food processor and grind until fine. In a cast-iron skillet, heat the canola oil to 325°F, or until the oil is bubbling. Remove the chicken from the buttermilk and dredge in the nut mixture until well coated. Fry the chicken in the hot oil for 4 to 5 minutes on each side, until golden brown. Transfer the chicken to paper towels to drain the excess oil. Serve with the sweet potatoes topped generously with the gravy.

MAKES 6 SERVINGS

 British extra special bitter

 Sauvignon Blanc

SMASHED SWEET POTATOES

3 large sweet potatoes, peeled and cut into 2-inch chunks

¼ cup firmly packed brown sugar

¼ cup pure maple syrup

8 tablespoons unsalted butter, cut into cubes

½ cup heavy cream

½ teaspoon sea salt

½ teaspoon freshly ground black pepper

Preheat the oven to 400°F. In a baking dish, combine the sweet potatoes, brown sugar, maple syrup, and butter and cover with foil. Bake for about 1½ hours, or until the potatoes are tender. Transfer the potatoes to a large bowl, reserving the leftover liquid. Using a mixer, beat the potatoes, adding a little reserved liquid until the potatoes are a smooth consistency. Add the cream, salt, and pepper and continue mixing until the potatoes are fluffy. If desired, the potatoes may be warmed over low heat in a heavy saucepan.

MAKES 6 SERVINGS

ASAP

At the heart of our region's farm-to-table movement is a dynamic organization called the Appalachian Sustainable Agriculture Project (ASAP), which promotes regional community-based foods that are locally owned and controlled, environmentally sound, economically viable, and health promoting. ASAP has been pivotal in establishing the area's wealth of farmers' and tailgate markets, family farm tours, school gardens, and a farm-to-hospital program. It also publishes a local food guide as well as The Mixing Bowl, a guide that our chefs use to source local produce.

Saltimbocca is Italian for "jumps in the mouth," and we think this Southern version will inspire you to take up mountain clogging, gee haw whimmy diddling, pottery-throwing, glass-blowing, and old-time fiddling. You may even begin inexplicably using the word y'all. Use high-quality country ham for the best results.

SOUTHERN CHICKEN SALTIMBOCCA WITH COUNTRY HAM IN A MUSHROOM MARSALA SAUCE

6 (6-ounce) boneless, skinless chicken breasts

1 cup plus 2 tablespoons all-purpose flour

2 cups olive oil

2 cups quartered cremini mushrooms (about 6 ounces mushrooms)

6 ounces thinly sliced country ham

6 slices thinly sliced provolone cheese

12 fresh sage leaves

½ cup marsala wine

1 cup chicken stock

⅔ cup demi-glace (page 13)

½ teaspoon sea salt

¼ teaspoon freshly ground black pepper

2 tablespoons unsalted butter

 Scottish ale

Chardonnay

Preheat the oven to 400°F. Dredge the chicken in 1 cup of the flour and set aside. In a skillet or sauté pan, heat the olive oil over medium heat to 325°F, or until the oil begins to bubble. Cook the chicken in the hot oil for 4 to 5 minutes, until it begins to brown. Turn the chicken over, add the mushrooms and country ham, and cook 4 to 5 minutes longer, until the chicken is golden brown. Remove the pan from the heat. With a slotted spoon, transfer the chicken to a baking dish, leaving the mushrooms and ham, and top each breast with a slice of the provolone and 2 sage leaves. Drain off the olive oil from the pan. Put the chicken in the oven for about 5 minutes, or until the cheese melts.

While the chicken is in the oven, add the remaining 2 tablespoons of flour to the mushroom and ham mixture and cook over medium heat for about 2 minutes, or until just thickened and the mushrooms are tender. Add the marsala wine to deglaze the pan, cooking over high heat and stirring to incorporate all of the pan drippings. Add the stock, demi-glace, salt, and pepper. Return the chicken to the skillet and cook over medium heat for about 2 minutes longer, or until the mixture is heated through. Transfer the chicken to a serving platter and finish the sauce by swirling the butter into the pan. Top the chicken with the sauce and serve immediately.

MAKES 6 SERVINGS

Why settle for a traditional boring meat loaf when you can make this piquant, flavorful masterpiece? Dried apples, poblano peppers, and the tarragon tomato flavors unite in a joyful composition of tartness, sweetness, and spiciness. Pickapeppa Sauce is made in Jamaica with tomatoes, raisins, mango, tamarind, and other spices and can be purchased at your local grocery. Goodness gracious.

CHICKEN APPLE MEAT LOAF WITH TARRAGON TOMATO GRAVY

1 tablespoon canola oil

1 cup diced celery

1 cup diced sweet onion (such as Vidalia; about 1 large onion)

1 pound ground chicken or turkey

1 egg

1 cup panko bread crumbs

1 cup diced dried apples (about 4 ounces dried apples)

½ cup diced poblano pepper

1¼ teaspoons sea salt

½ teaspoon freshly ground black pepper

3 tablespoons Pickapeppa Sauce

Tarragon Tomato Gravy (recipe follows)

Preheat the oven to 350°F. Heat the canola oil in a medium sauté pan or skillet over medium heat. Sauté the celery and onion for about 5 minutes, or until just tender. In a bowl, combine the chicken, egg, bread crumbs, apples, poblano pepper, the sautéed vegetables, salt, and pepper. Form the mixture into a loaf shape and put in a 9 by 13-inch baking pan. Cover the top of the meat loaf with the Pickapeppa Sauce and bake, uncovered, for about 1 hour, or until browned on top with an internal temperature of 160°F. Serve with the warm gravy.

MAKES 4 SERVINGS

brown ale

Rioja, Chardonnay

TARRAGON TOMATO GRAVY

1 tablespoon chopped fresh
    tarragon

½ cup demi-glace (page 13)

1 (14-ounce) can stewed
    tomatoes

¼ teaspoon sea salt

¼ teaspoon freshly ground
    black pepper

In a heavy saucepan, combine the tarragon, demi-glace, tomatoes, and salt. Bring to a boil over high heat and immediately reduce the heat to low to simmer for about 20 minutes, or until the mixture coats the back of a spoon. Add the pepper the last minute of cooking time. Serve immediately.

MAKES 2 CUPS

"When my grandmother wanted chicken and dumplings, my sister and I were sent to do battle in the hen yard. Brandishing little rods with crookneck ends, we felt like Roman soldiers among the Sabines."

—Bill Neal, *Southern Cooking*

We say it often in Asheville: We applaud eclecticism. This recipe reflects that. Take some citrusy Latin-flavored heat, add some Cajun sausage, and stir-fry it all Chinese style. It's sophisticated, worldly chicken with an attitude.

CHICKEN ANDOUILLE STIR-FRY WITH ORANGE JALAPEÑO GLAZE

½ cup canola oil

2 pounds boneless, skinless chicken breasts, cut into 1- to 2-inch pieces

½ teaspoon sea salt

1 pound andouille sausage, sliced into ¼-inch pieces

1 large green bell pepper, seeded and cut into 1-inch pieces

1 large red bell pepper, seeded and cut into 1-inch pieces

1 large yellow bell pepper, seeded and cut into 1-inch pieces

1 cup chopped celery (about 4 celery ribs)

2 cups chopped Vidalia onion (about 2 large onions)

1½ cups freshly squeezed orange juice

2 tablespoons cornstarch

3 tablespoons green jalapeño hot sauce

½ teaspoon freshly ground black pepper

Heat the canola oil over medium-high heat in a large sauté pan or skillet. Sprinkle the chicken with salt and add to the oil. Cook, stirring constantly, for 2 to 3 minutes, until the chicken begins to brown. Add the sausage, green bell pepper, red bell pepper, yellow bell pepper, celery, and onion and cook for 12 to 14 minutes longer, until the chicken is cooked through and the vegetables are tender. In a bowl, combine the orange juice, cornstarch, jalapeño hot sauce, and black pepper until the cornstarch is dissolved. Add the orange juice mixture to the chicken and vegetables and cook for 2 to 3 minutes longer, until the sauce thickens.

MAKES 6 TO 8 SERVINGS

American pale ale

Garnacha, Gewürztraminer

This savory, herb-i-licious chicken is what we call honest food: straightforward, authentic, genuine love from the kitchen. It's the kind of food your mom and your grandmom used to make before everything had to be encrusted or encased or enveloped in some elaborate way. It may be unpretentious in its presentation, but it's delicious enough for any holiday table.

HERB-ROASTED WHOLE CHICKEN WITH SAVORY PAN GRAVY

STUFFING

2 cups peeled, diced carrots (3 or 4 large carrots)

2 cups diced celery (about 8 celery ribs)

2 cups diced Vidalia onion (about 2 onions)

2 tablespoons chopped fresh thyme

2 tablespoons chopped fresh sage

2 tablespoons chopped fresh basil

2 tablespoons chopped fresh rosemary

2 teaspoons sea salt

1 teaspoon freshly ground black pepper

½ cup olive oil

1 (3-pound) chicken

SAVORY PAN GRAVY

Backbone from the roasted chicken

Vegetable mix and giblets from the roasting pan

2 cups plus 2 tablespoons water

2 tablespoons cornstarch

 Scottish ale, American pale ale

Rioja, Chardonnay

Preheat the oven to 350°F. To make the stuffing, combine all the ingredients in a large bowl.

Remove the giblets from the chicken and set aside. Stuff the cavity of the chicken with the vegetable and herb mixture until the cavity is packed full. In a large roasting pan, put the giblets in the bottom and add any leftover vegetable mix. Place the chicken on top of the giblets and vegetables. Rub the chicken with leftover oil from the bowl and roast for about 1 hour and 40 minutes, or until the juices run clear. Let the chicken rest while you make the gravy, keeping the chicken warm by tenting with aluminum foil.

To make the gravy, stand the roasted chicken upright and with a sharp knife, cut down each side of the backbone to remove the bone. In a saucepan, combine the backbone, vegetable mix and giblets, and 2 cups of the water. Bring to a boil and immediately decrease the heat to medium. Simmer, skimming off the oil from the top of the stock, for about 20 minutes, or until the liquid is reduced by one-fourth. Mix the cornstarch with the remaining 2 tablespoons water. Increase the heat to high and bring the stock to a boil, stirring in the cornstarch mixture, and cook for about 2 minutes, or until thickened. With a sieve, strain and discard the solids and pour the gravy into a serving bowl. Serve warm over the roasted chicken.

MAKES 4 SERVINGS

Most of us think of the freezer aisle in the grocery store when we think about chicken potpie, but this pie made from scratch is comfort food. Jazzy comfort food with a touch of the Caribbean, with a hint of coconut. The blackening flavors are also unusual and unexpected in a chicken potpie. This recipe takes a little time, but your family and friends will thank you.

BLACKENED CHICKEN POTPIE

4 (6-ounce) boneless, skinless chicken breasts

¼ cup plus 2 tablespoons canola oil

4 tablespoons Blackening Spice (recipe follows)

2 cups chopped Vidalia onion (about 2 large onions)

2 cups chopped celery (about 8 celery ribs)

2 cups peeled and chopped red potatoes (about 3 large potatoes)

2 cups peeled and chopped carrots (about 4 large carrots)

1 cup diced poblano pepper (about 2 large poblano peppers)

⅔ cup all-purpose flour

2 cups chicken stock

¾ cup coconut milk

2 tablespoons minced hot cherry peppers

2 tablespoons Worcestershire Sauce

1 teaspoon chopped fresh thyme

1¼ teaspoons sea salt

1 teaspoon freshly ground black pepper

Pie Dough (recipe follows; use doubled)

Belgian Saison

Gewürztraminer

Preheat a cast iron-skillet on high heat. Rub the chicken breasts with 2 tablespoons of the canola oil. Coat the breasts with the spice mixture. Place the chicken in the hot skillet and cook quickly, 4 to 5 minutes per side. Remove the chicken from the skillet and transfer to a bowl to cool.

Preheat the oven to 400°F. Heat the remaining ¼ cup canola oil in a large heavy-bottomed pan over high heat. Add the onion, celery, potatoes, carrots, and poblano pepper and cook, stirring occasionally, for 15 to 20 minutes, until the poblano is just tender. Decrease the heat to medium and stir in the flour until well combined, cooking for about 3 minutes, or until just thickened. Add the stock, coconut milk, cherry peppers, Worcestershire, thyme, salt, and pepper and cook for about 10 minutes, or until the mixture is thickened. Cut the chicken into 1-inch cubes and add to the filling mixture, along with any chicken juices left in the bowl. Mix all the ingredients until well combined.

Butter 2 (9-inch) deep-dish pie pans. Roll out 4 (10-inch) pie crusts. Place a crust in each pan. Pour the chicken mixture into the pans and top each with another round of dough. Crimp the edges of the pies with a fork. Bake for 45 to 50 minutes, until golden brown.

MAKES 2 PIES; 8 SERVINGS

BLACKENING SPICE

1 tablespoon sugar

1 tablespoon sea salt

1 teaspoon freshly ground
black pepper

1 teaspoon cayenne pepper

1 tablespoon smoked paprika

1 teaspoon powdered onion

1 teaspoon powdered garlic

1 teaspoon dried thyme

½ teaspoon dried oregano

Combine all the ingredients in a large bowl and use as blackening spice for poultry, fish, or beef.

MAKES ½ CUP

PIE DOUGH

2½ cups all-purpose flour

1 teaspoon sea salt

1 teaspoon sugar

1 cup cold unsalted butter,
cut into pieces

½ cup ice water

In a food processor, combine the flour, salt, and sugar. Add the butter and pulse until the mixture resembles coarse meal, about 10 seconds. Add the ice water in a slow stream, pulsing the mixture no more than 30 seconds, until it begins to form a ball. Remove the dough from the processor and divide into 2 pieces. Wrap each piece in plastic wrap and flatten with the palm of your hand. Refrigerate for at least 1 hour. When ready to use, roll out each piece on a floured surface using a floured rolling pin to make 2 pie crusts.

MAKES 2 (9 OR 10-INCH) CRUSTS

BEYOND THE SMOKEHOUSE

Buttermilk Pork Chops with Creamy Red-Eye Gravy

Parsley-Crusted Lamb Chops with Dijon Demi-Glace

Root Beer Molasses–Glazed Pork Tenderloin with Smoked Jalapeño Sauce and Apple Salsa

Lamb and Multi-Mushroom Meat Loaf with Mint Glaze

Beef Tenderloin Wrapped in Maple-Peppered Bacon with Gorgonzola Gratinée and Green Peppercorn Bordelaise Sauce

Pork and Blueberry Sausage Simmered in Maple Syrup

Char-Grilled Pork Tenderloin with Peach Fennel Salsa

Pan-Fried Pork Chops with Black-Eyed Pea and Andouille Sausage Ragout

Smoked Jalapeño–Glazed New York Strip Steak with Tomato Shallot Gravy

Lamb and Root Vegetable Stew Topped with Grits Croutons

The smokehouse is an iconic fixture in the southern Appalachian region, its utilitarian reputation the result of needing to put aside meat for the winter months. Ever scrappy and frugal, early Blue Ridge settlers would butcher hogs at the first cold snap in the fall and put aside meat, rubbed with salt and spices, to cure. Today's modern chefs are rediscovering the rewards of a well-run smokehouse and many are curing their own hams and bacon, making their own sausages, prosciutto, and salami.

Lamb and mutton are other mountain staples, although mutton, with its strong taste, doesn't make it to today's table very often. We do, however, love the flavors of lamb mingled with rosemary, combined with wild mushrooms from the Blue Ridge, and paired with root vegetables, which grow so well in the region. We are also proud of the beef we serve at Tupelo Honey Cafe, made from local grass-fed cattle. We're big fans of Hickory Nut Gap Farm just east of Asheville, whose proprietors, the Ager and Clark families, have been farming in their idyllic valley for multiple generations.

Our fun comes from taking great cuts of beef, pork, and lamb and marrying them with the flavors from our larder: Char-Grilled Pork Tenderloin with Peach Fennel Salsa, Root Beer Molasses–Glazed Pork Tenderloin with Smoked Jalapeño Sauce and Apple Salsa, and Smoked Jalapeño–Glazed New York Strip Steak with Tomato Shallot Gravy. We also delight in a little element of surprise—meat loaf ratcheted up by using lamb, or sausage made with pork and blueberries from our farm. You can be creative, too, with flavor combinations, so don't be afraid to experiment a little.

"Yet the demand is . . . being met with the renaissance of the farmers' markets. Town, county, and state governments wisely support and encourage small rural farmers to get the best of their produce to the local populace. Only a person without a soul would not revel in these affairs. Ham and sausage biscuits and fried peach and apple pies are the hearty breakfasts awaiting the daybreaking souls who know to arrive punctually . . . And for the true shopper, the ultimate satisfaction, a glib "you should have been here earlier for the baby okra" to a late-arriving neighbor."

—Bill Neal, *Southern Cooking*

If (heaven forbid) you do not own a cast-iron skillet, this recipe alone is worth the investment. The best cast-iron skillets have been used over decades and have retained the goodness of every meal in the process, culinary ghostly inhabitants of many a family supper. Soaking the pork chops in buttermilk renders them juicy, tender, and succulent.

BUTTERMILK PORK CHOPS
WITH CREAMY RED-EYE GRAVY

8 (½ to ¾ inch thick) bone-in pork chops

2 cups buttermilk

2 cups canola oil

4 cups all-purpose flour

1½ teaspoons sea salt

1 tablespoon freshly ground black pepper

1½ cups Creamy Red-Eye Gravy (page 12)

Place the pork chops in a large nonreactive container, cover with buttermilk, and marinate overnight in the refrigerator. Remove the chops from the refrigerator and discard the buttermilk. Heat the canola oil in a cast-iron skillet over medium heat until just bubbling, or about 325°F. Combine the flour, salt, and pepper and mix well. Dredge the pork chops in the flour mixture until well coated on both sides. Cook in the oil for 3 to 4 minutes on each side, until done in the middle. Serve with the gravy.

MAKES 4 SERVINGS

Porter

Zinfandel

We get fantastic grass-fed lamb chops from our area farmers and wouldn't dream of violating their integrity with overpreparation. You want these to be cooked quickly over high heat so they are pink in the middle and the Dijon has just begun to permeate the meat with its Dijon-ness. These call for a deep, jammy Cabernet Sauvignon.

PARSLEY CRUSTED LAMB CHOPS WITH DIJON DEMI-GLACE

2 cups panko bread crumbs

2 tablespoons minced fresh parsley

¼ teaspoon sea salt

¼ teaspoon freshly ground black pepper

½ cup canola oil

4 (1½ to 2 inches thick) lamb chops

3 tablespoons whole-grain Dijon mustard

2 cups demi-glace (page 13)

Combine the bread crumbs, parsley, salt, and pepper in a food processor and pulse until fine. Heat the canola oil in a heavy skillet over medium heat until the oil is 350°F on a deep-fat thermometer. Rub the lamb chops with 2 tablespoons of the mustard and then dredge each in the crumb mixture until well coated. Cook the lamb in hot oil for 2 to 3 minutes on each side, until the lamb reaches 140°F. In a small saucepan, combine the demi-glace and the remaining 1 tablespoon mustard over high heat. Serve the sauce immediately spooned over the lamb chops.

MAKES 2 SERVINGS

Scottish ale, French Bière de Garde

Cabernet Sauvignon

Your taste buds may never be the same after this explosion of flavors. Your palate will thank you for stocking your larder, and family and friends will be hypnotically lured into your kitchen as you finish this entrée with a touch of jalapeño heat and tart apple. The root beer's promise of sassafras plus the mellow taste of molasses equals an Appalachian mountain kiss.

ROOT BEER MOLASSES–GLAZED PORK TENDERLOIN WITH SMOKED JALAPEÑO SAUCE AND APPLE SALSA

1 pork tenderloin (about 1 pound)

12 ounces root beer

½ cup molasses

1 tablespoon canola oil

½ cup Smoked Jalapeño Sauce (page 23)

2 cups Apple Salsa (page 4)

Cut the tenderloin diagonally into 1-inch-thick slices and set aside. In a medium bowl, combine the root beer and molasses, mixing thoroughly. Pour over the pork loin. Cover and marinate for at least 1 hour. Heat the canola oil in a large heavy skillet over high heat until the oil is 350°F on a deep-fat thermometer. Drain and discard the liquid from the pork and place the pork slices in the hot oil, searing for about 3 minutes on each side, or until cooked to medium. Serve immediately drizzled with the jalapeño sauce and topped with the salsa.

MAKES 4 SERVINGS

 Altbier, Oktoberfest Marzen

Riesling

Beyond the Smokehouse

149

In the Blue Ridge Mountains, mutton and lamb have long been a staple and hardy livestock perfectly suited for our hilly and sometimes rocky terrain. And hunting and collecting wild mushrooms in our forests and fields has brought sexy back to mycology. The marriage of these two earthy ingredients creates a comfort food that makes your run-of-the-mill meat loaf pale by comparison. Mint is a classic complement to lamb.

LAMB AND MULTI-MUSHROOM MEAT LOAF WITH MINT GLAZE

1 tablespoon canola oil

1 cup diced Vidalia onion (about 1 large onion)

1 cup diced celery (about 4 celery ribs)

4 ounces sliced mushrooms (such as shiitakes or morels)

1 pound ground lamb

¾ teaspoon sea salt

1 teaspoon freshly ground black pepper

2 eggs

1 tablespoon low-sodium soy sauce

¾ cup crumbled Ritz Crackers

4 cups demi-glace (page 13)

2 tablespoons minced fresh mint

Preheat the oven to 450°F. Heat the canola oil in a sauté pan or skillet over medium-high heat and sauté the onion, celery, and mushrooms for about 10 minutes, or until tender. In a bowl, combine the lamb, vegetable mixture, salt, pepper, eggs, soy sauce, and crackers and mix thoroughly. In a casserole dish, form the meat mixture into a tight loaf and cover with foil.

Bake for about 40 minutes, remove the foil, and drain off the excess oil. Continue baking uncovered for 10 minutes longer, or until the top of the loaf is brown.

In a medium saucepan, combine the demi-glace and mint and simmer over low heat until hot. Serve with the meat loaf.

MAKES 6 TO 8 SERVINGS

dark Belgian Trappist

Chianti

Turkeys & Pigs

Pigs don't sweat! They roll in mud to cool off!

Piglets love to play with balls and eachother!

Pig manure is high in nitrogen & makes excellent fertilizer.

plow!

Pigs can run 11 miles per hour!

Hickory Nut Gap Meats

Jamie Ager is a fourth-generation farmer at Hickory Nut Gap, and his beef, lamb, pork, and poultry are much sought after by area chefs for their taste and quality. Rotational grazing and grass-fed livestock practices result in superior meats at Hickory Nut. Jamie's ninety-acre family homestead, which is worked along with his mom and dad, also includes ten acres of apple orchards and six hundred laying hens. Jamie's cousin, Annie Louise Perkinson, and her husband, Isaiah, oversee Flying Cloud farm, an adjoining eleven-acre organic vegetable and fruit farm, selling at farmers' markets as well as membership in their CSA.

If you decide to treat yourself to this amazing entrée, under no circumstances should you take short cuts with the ingredients. Buy the best beef you can, seek out the maple-peppered bacon, and invest in high-quality gorgonzola. Open a bottle of fruity Zinfandel or a sultry Cabernet Sauvignon and enjoy.

BEEF TENDERLOIN WRAPPED IN MAPLE-PEPPERED BACON WITH GORGONZOLA GRATINÉE AND GREEN PEPPERCORN BORDELAISE SAUCE

½ cup demi-glace (page 13)

2 tablespoons tomato puree

1 tablespoon green peppercorns

2 (2 to 3 inches thick) beef tenderloin steaks

⅛ teaspoon sea salt

⅛ teaspoon freshly ground black pepper

2 strips maple-peppered bacon

3 ounces gorgonzola cheese, crumbled

To make the green peppercorn bordelaise sauce, combine the demi-glace, tomato puree, and peppercorns in a small saucepan over low heat.

Preheat the grill to medium-high. Season the tenderloins with salt and pepper and then wrap them with the bacon, securing with toothpicks. Cook the steaks for 4 to 5 minutes per side, until medium rare, and transfer to a serving platter. Top each steak with one-half of the gorgonzola and place briefly under the broiler, or just until the cheese begins to melt. Transfer the steaks to plates and drizzle with the peppercorn sauce.

MAKES 2 SERVINGS

extra special bitter

Zinfandel, Cabernet Sauvignon

A scrumptious centerpiece for brunch (along with a full stack of buttermilk pancakes or a basket of buttermilk biscuits), this lovely concoction is deceptively simple to make and yet so rewarding. We offer it here as an entrée because it is also delicious as a Sunday night supper with your favorite omelet.

PORK AND BLUEBERRY SAUSAGE SIMMERED IN MAPLE SYRUP

1 pound freshly ground pork sausage

½ cup dried blueberries

½ cup pure maple syrup (no substitutes here!)

Mix the sausage and blueberries together and form into 10 sausage balls. Over medium heat, cook the sausage balls in a nonstick skillet, turning them every other minute for 6 to 7 minutes, until browned on all sides. Add the maple syrup and bring to a simmer, continuing to cook for 1 minute. Stir or roll around the balls while simmering so they're coated all over. Transfer the sausage balls to a serving platter. Strain the syrup mixture, pour over the sausage balls, and serve.

MAKES 4 TO 6 SERVINGS

 Belgian Saison, Belgian pale ale

old vine Zinfandel

Certainly a summer grill-out favorite, there's something about this recipe that also says autumn to us. In the Blue Ridge, we have mild autumn days (and exquisite foliage colored gold, orange, russet, and eggplant), often until the end of November, and this dish is a great way to bid your grill a fond farewell for the season. It's also an imaginative alternative to the traditional Thanksgiving turkey dinner.

CHAR-GRILLED PORK TENDERLOIN WITH PEACH FENNEL SALSA

4½ teaspoons minced fresh
    rosemary leaves

2 tablespoons olive oil

1 tablespoon Worcestershire
    Sauce

1 teaspoon sea salt

2 teaspoons freshly ground
    black pepper

1 pork tenderloin (about
    1 pound)

1 cup Peach Fennel Salsa
    (page 5)

Preheat your grill to medium-high. Combine the rosemary, olive oil, Worcestershire, salt, and pepper in a large bowl. Place the pork in the bowl, covering it well with the rosemary mixture, and set aside for 30 minutes. Cook the pork loin on the grill for 12 to 14 minutes, until medium, turning every couple of minutes to ensure it cooks evenly. Remove the pork from the heat and slice into 1-inch-thick pieces, topping each with the salsa.

MAKES 2 SERVINGS

  German Altbier, French Bière de Garde

Carménerè

Any true Southerner will remind you that eating black-eyed peas will bring you good luck, especially if you eat them with collard or turnip greens (which bring you money) on New Year's Day. We add a touch of Louisiana to our ragout with delicious andouille and poof! Our luck has changed for the better already.

PAN-FRIED PORK CHOPS WITH BLACK-EYED PEA AND ANDOUILLE SAUSAGE RAGOUT

2 tablespoons canola oil

8 (½ to 1 inch thick) bone-in pork chops

1 teaspoon sea salt

1 teaspoon freshly ground black pepper

2 tablespoons marsala wine

Andouille Sausage Ragout (recipe follows)

Heat the canola oil in a heavy skillet over high heat until the oil is 350°F on a deep-fat thermometer. Season the pork chops with salt and pepper and place in the hot oil, cooking about 3 minutes per side, or until the chops are cooked through. Deglaze the pan with the marsala and serve the chops over the ragout.

MAKES 4 SERVINGS

pale ale

Pinot Noir, Chardonnay

ANDOUILLE SAUSAGE RAGOUT

1 tablespoon canola oil

1½ teaspoons minced garlic

6 ounces andouille sausage, diced

1½ cups diced Vidalia onion (about 2 medium onions)

1½ cups diced celery (about 6 celery ribs)

1½ cups peeled, diced carrot (5 or 6 large carrots)

½ cup marsala wine

1 cup demi-glace (page 13)

1 (14-ounce) can black-eyed peas, thoroughly drained

1 teaspoon minced fresh rosemary

1 teaspoon minced fresh sage

1 teaspoon minced fresh thyme

For the ragout, in a heavy saucepan over high heat, combine the canola oil, garlic, and andouille sausage and cook for about 5 minutes, or until the sausage is browned. Decrease the heat to medium and add the onion, celery, and carrots and cook for about 10 minutes, or until the vegetables are softened. Deglaze the pan with the marsala wine. Add the demi-glace, peas, rosemary, sage, and thyme and simmer for about 10 minutes so that all the flavors combine.

Elevate your strip steak to new heights. Ideal for game day fare or a summer cookout with the neighborhood. Be sure you have plenty of the Tomato Shallot Gravy on hand in case you want to add a side of mashed potatoes or Goat Cheese Basil Grits (page 179).

SMOKED JALAPEÑO–GLAZED NEW YORK STRIP STEAK WITH TOMATO SHALLOT GRAVY

2 (2 inches thick) New York strip steaks

1 cup Smoked Jalapeño Sauce (page 23)

¾ cup Tomato Shallot Gravy (page 16)

 brown ale

Cabernet Sauvignon

Preheat your grill to high. Rub the steaks with about ¼ cup of the sauce and place the meat on the grill. Glaze the steaks with the remaining sauce, using a basting brush, while cooking to your desired state of wellness. We recommend 6 minutes per side for medium rare. Serve with the gravy.

MAKES 2 SERVINGS

Tailgate Markets

The Mountain Tailgate Market Association cultivates over sixteen farmers' markets in a two-county area in western North Carolina, including a delightful one right in downtown—the Asheville City Market. The market features local food from local farmers, including produce, local eggs, meats and fish, brick-oven breads, handmade pasta, fruit butters, preserves, mountain herbs and flowers, and gourmet cheeses. The market runs from April until the end of November and is open Wednesdays and Saturdays.

Lexigton Ave. curb market c. 1970

We like to make this comforting stew in the fall and winter, particularly on cold and blustery days when the fireplace beckons and you want something savory, flavorful, and hearty. Nutritious root vegetables have long been a staple of the Appalachian kitchen in winter, and this stew pulls them out of the humble obscurity of the root cellar and places them into the spotlight they so richly deserve.

LAMB AND ROOT VEGETABLE STEW TOPPED WITH GRITS CROUTONS

1 tablespoon olive oil

1½ pounds lamb leg or shoulder, cut into 1-inch cubes, bones reserved

1 cup chopped Vidalia onion (about 1 large onion)

1 cup chopped celery (about 4 celery ribs)

1 cup peeled, chopped carrots (about 2 large carrots)

1 cup peeled, chopped sweet potato (about 1 large potato)

1 cup peeled, chopped Irish potato (about 1 large potato)

1 cup chopped turnip (about 1 large turnip)

1 cup chopped rutabaga (about 2 medium rutabagas)

1 cup chopped parsnip (about 2 large parsnips)

1 teaspoon sea salt

2 teaspoons freshly ground black pepper

1 tablespoon minced fresh rosemary

2 teaspoons minced fresh thyme

1 teaspoon minced fresh sage

4 cups demi-glace (page 13)

Tupelo Honey Ginormous Biscuits (page 189)

Irish stout

Cabernet Sauvignon

Heat the olive oil in a heavy-bottomed stockpot over high heat until the oil is 350°F on a deep-fat thermometer and add the lamb, along with the bones, searing for about 10 minutes, or until browned on all sides. Add the onion and cook for about 3 minutes longer, or until the onion is caramelized. Add the celery, carrots, sweet potato, Irish potato, turnip, rutabaga, parsnip, salt, and pepper, cooking for 10 minutes longer, stirring often, or until caramelized.

Remove the bones from the pot and scrape out the marrow, returning the marrow to the stew. Add the rosemary, thyme, sage, and 2 cups of the demi-glace and bring to a boil before reducing to a simmer. Continue to add the remaining 2 cups of the demi-glace ½ cup at a time while the ragout cooks for about 1 hour, or until the lamb is tender. Serve with the biscuits.

MAKES 8 SERVINGS

THE
THREES

Benne-Coated Asparagus

Tupelo Honey Pickled Beet Salad

Macaroni and Gouda Casserole

Mondo Mushroom Ragout

Beets My Heart

Cheesy Mashed Cauliflower

Tupelo Honey–Glazed Carrots

Fried Green Tomatoes with
Goat Cheese Basil Grits

Salsa Verde Pinto Beans

Candied-Ginger Cornbread Dressing

In the South, you may sometimes be confused about the meal you're about to eat. That's because we call *lunch* "dinner" and sometimes call *dinner* "supper." Of course, none of these is the same as *Sunday dinner*, a postchurch spread designed to impress friends, family, and clergy and guaranteed to bring on the other Southern Sunday tradition known as the *Sunday afternoon nap*. The more cosmopolitan Southerner now partakes of the *Sunday brunch* (which is discussed in the next chapter), mainly, we believe, because we just can't get enough breakfast, regardless of the time of day.

At any rate, our midday meal often draws inspiration from our agrarian roots, when men would come in from working the farm in the middle of the day and need significant fortifying to go back out and finish their chores. Thus, the concept of *meat and three* was born: a meal consisting of a meat of some sort and then three vegetable or complementary sides. It was a popular idea, naturally, and commercial diners and mom and pop restaurants embraced the idea of a daily offering of some sort of assortment of three sides to go with a) meat loaf, fried chicken, or pork chop and/or b) a large slab of cornbread or basket of biscuits.

We honor this heritage at Tupelo Honey Cafe, not only because we think it's a grand tradition and a good idea, but because we love the color and freshness and vitamin-packed flavors of fresh vegetables. We also believe that there should be more respect for a plate of vegetable trinity; on the menu ours can stand alone as a delicious meal. Just remember, the sometimes maligned vegetables, like cauliflower or beets, as examples, are often undiscovered culinary stars, as you'll see in the following recipes. Humble beginnings perhaps. But with the right preparation, revered enough for the Sunday table.

"Sweet potatoes are to the . . . country cooking of the South what beans are to Boston: a signature dish of symbolic importance and great public favor."

—John Egerton, Southern Food

The slight nuttiness of sesame—a Low Country influence, where benne (sesame seeds) were introduced to coastal Carolina and Georgia through trade with Africa—is lovely with fresh asparagus. As a matter of fact, if you're visiting our coastal cousins, be sure you try some benne seed wafers or cookies. Delicious. Fresh asparagus has a natural place in each stem where the bottom of the stalk breaks off. Simply hold the stalk in the middle and bend the lower half of the asparagus until the tougher, more bitter end of the stalk breaks.

BENNE-COATED ASPARAGUS

3 pounds trimmed asparagus

2 tablespoons sesame oil

2 teaspoons sea salt

1 tablespoon freshly ground black pepper

3 tablespoons sesame seeds

Blanch the asparagus in salted boiling water for 2 to 3 minutes, just until tender. In a large sauté pan or skillet, heat the sesame oil over medium-high heat and add the asparagus, cooking 2 to 3 minutes, until hot. Add the salt, pepper, and sesame seeds for the last minute of cooking.

MAKES 8 SERVINGS

Asheville City Hall c. 1892

With its deep red beets, this salad is as beautiful as it is delicious. You can also use an assortment of different colored fresh beets—golden, orange, purple—if you want to really dazzle the crowd. Try this as a different type of side with your next cheeseburger.

TUPELO HONEY PICKLED BEET SALAD

2 pounds beets

1 large Vidalia onion

2 cloves garlic

¾ cup olive oil

1 cup cider vinegar

½ cup tupelo honey

2 teaspoons sea salt

1 teaspoon ground white pepper

Peel and trim the beets and onion, slice very thin using a mandoline or food processor, and transfer to a large bowl. With the flat side of a knife, crush the garlic cloves and add whole to the beet and onion mixture. In a medium bowl, combine the olive oil, vinegar, honey, salt, and white pepper and pour over the beets. Mix well, cover, and refrigerate overnight before serving.

MAKES 8 TO 10 SERVINGS

Okay, so technically speaking, mac and cheese isn't actually a vegetable, but it's generally considered a vegetable side in the South. Vegetable or no, it's an important part of our Southern culinary vernacular. Just be aware this rich version will quickly become a favorite at your table, and you may never return to the standard mac and cheese in a box. It's also great on its own as an entrée with an arugula and walnut salad and some fresh fruit.

MACARONI AND GOUDA CHEESE CASSEROLE

4 ounces Ritz Crackers

1 cup panko bread crumbs

1½ teaspoons sea salt

1 teaspoon freshly ground black pepper

2 tablespoons unsalted butter, melted

1 teaspoon olive oil

1 large sweet onion (such as Vidalia), diced

8 cups water

2 cups elbow macaroni

3 cups heavy cream

1½ cups shredded gouda cheese (about 8 ounces cheese)

1 tablespoon Worcestershire Sauce

1 tablespoon green hot pepper sauce

½ cup grated Parmesan cheese

Preheat the oven to 400°F. Lightly butter a 9 by 13-inch baking dish. In a food processor, pulse the crackers, bread crumbs, ½ teaspoon of the salt, and ½ teaspoon of the pepper, until coarsely ground. Place the mixture in a large bowl and combine with the melted butter. Set the cracker mixture aside.

Heat the olive oil and the onion in a medium skillet over medium-high heat for 5 to 6 minutes, until the onion is translucent. Bring the water to a boil in a large stockpot and add ½ teaspoon of the salt. Add the macaroni and cook over high heat for about 12 minutes, or until just tender or al dente. Drain the pasta and return to the stockpot. Add the onion, cream, gouda cheese, Worcestershire, hot pepper sauce, and the remaining ½ teaspoon salt and ½ teaspoon pepper. Cook over high heat, stirring frequently, for about 5 minutes. or until the cheese is melted.

Sprinkle half of the bread crumb mixture evenly on the bottom of the prepared baking dish. Pour in the macaroni mixture and top with the remaining bread crumb mixture. Sprinkle the Parmesan cheese on top and bake for about 15 minutes, or until golden brown. Turn the oven off and let the casserole rest inside for 5 minutes before serving.

MAKES 8 TO 12 SERVINGS

This earthy, herby ragout is the perfect accompaniment to just about any type of meat, but we're especially fond of pairing this with beef and pork. The flavors meld perfectly and add an element of wonderful flavor to the accompanying mashed sweet or Irish potatoes. We like to use a combination of cremini, oyster, shiitake, and portobello mushrooms in making this dish, but you can play with the right mushroom equation for your personal taste.

MONDO MUSHROOM RAGOUT

2 tablespoons olive oil

6 cloves garlic, minced

6 shallots, peeled and quartered

1 large Vidalia onion, chopped

3 pounds mushrooms, trimmed
   (see headnote)

2 cups dry red wine

2 cups demi-glace (page 13)

2 teaspoons minced fresh
   rosemary

2 teaspoons minced fresh
   thyme

1 teaspoon minced fresh sage

1 teaspoon minced fresh
   oregano

1 teaspoon sea salt

2 teaspoons freshly ground
   black pepper

Heat the olive oil in a heavy stockpot over high heat. Sauté the garlic, shallots, and onion for about 2 minutes, or until the vegetables are softened and caramelized. Add the mushrooms and cook for about 10 minutes, or until the mushrooms are tender. Add the wine to deglaze the pan and cook for 10 minutes longer. Add the demi-glace, rosemary, thyme, sage, oregano, salt, and pepper and bring to a boil. Lower the heat and simmer for 45 minutes to 1 hour, or until the mixture thickens.

MAKES 6 TO 8 SERVINGS

Shoo-Mercy

This is one of those Tupelo Honey Cafe urban myths. No one is quite sure how it got started, but it implies bounty—lots and lots of bounty. Take, for example, a breakfast order of eggs, sausage, and biscuits. If it's a Shoo-Mercy order, you basically get twice as much. Shrimp and grits? Twice as many shrimp. So, it's a descriptor that's tough to define except that it makes you very, very happy.

For some reason, beets frighten people. So do turnips. And parsnips. Why, you ask? They've simply gotten a bad rap. But trust us. The combination of these vitamin-packed root vegetables with cream and simple seasoning creates a memorable side to roast pork or chicken or a standing beef rib roast.

BEETS MY HEART

2 pounds beets, peeled and diced

1 pound turnips, peeled and diced

½ pound parsnips, peeled and diced

2 tablespoons olive oil

1 teaspoon sea salt

1 teaspoon freshly ground black pepper

1 cup heavy cream, or as needed

Preheat the oven to 400°F. Toss the beets, turnips, and parsnips in the olive oil and sprinkle with the salt and pepper. Place the vegetables in a shallow baking dish, cover with foil, and bake for 45 minutes to 1 hour, or until tender. Transfer the vegetables to a heavy large pan and add the cream. Over medium-high heat, cook the mixture for about 15 minutes, or until the cream is reduced by half. Puree the mixture, while still hot, in batches if necessary, in a food processor until smooth. Add additional cream, 1 tablespoon at a time, if the mixture is too thick. Serve immediately.

MAKES 8 SERVINGS

We serve this side at the restaurant in place of mashed potatoes, and sworn cauliflower-haters are immediate converts. It's hilarious, in fact, to tell someone he's eating cauliflower and watch the look of surprise on his face. The texture of the dish is meant to be a little chunky, a little funky, and surprisingly tasty.

CHEESY MASHED CAULIFLOWER

2 large heads cauliflower, cored and broken into florets

4 ounces cream cheese

1¼ cups shredded sharp cheddar cheese (about 6 ounces cheese)

2 teaspoons roasted garlic puree (page 5)

¼ teaspoon sea salt

⅛ teaspoon freshly ground black pepper

⅛ teaspoon freshly ground white pepper

2 teaspoons unsalted butter

Steam the cauliflower for 10 to 12 minutes, until just tender. Place the cauliflower in a large bowl and mash with a potato masher or fork. In another large bowl, combine the cream cheese, cheddar cheese, garlic puree, salt, black pepper, white pepper, and butter. Pour the hot mashed cauliflower on top of the cheese mixture and combine, using a large spoon, until the cheeses are thoroughly melted. Serve immediately.

MAKES 8 TO 10 SERVINGS

So sweet and simple. We're partial to tupelo honey, but our mountain region is abundant with various nuanced honeys—from sourwood to wildflower—and each one can lend a slightly different flavor and aroma to this dish. These carrots are exquisitely beautiful, too, paired with our Herb-Roasted Whole Chicken with Savory Pan Gravy (page 136).

TUPELO HONEY–GLAZED CARROTS

2 pounds young, slender carrots, tops removed, peeled

2 tablespoons unsalted butter

1 teaspoon sea salt

1 teaspoon freshly ground black pepper

3 heaping tablespoons artisanal honey (such as tupelo honey)

Blanch the carrots in salted boiling water for about 7 minutes, or until just tender. Drain off the liquid. In a large sauté pan or skillet, melt the butter and add the carrots, salt, and pepper, Cook for about 3 minutes, or until heated through, before adding the honey. Coat the carrots with the honey by stirring the mixture for 1 to 2 minutes and serve immediately.

MAKES 8 SERVINGS

We have no idea what resourceful, innovative home cook first had the idea of using up a bumper crop of tomatoes by picking them green and frying them. Likely it was somebody weary of canning all August and September. Regardless, she should be thanked. A staple of many Southern tables, particularly during summer and early fall, these savory slices of tartness are perfect with the creamy tanginess of our grits made with local goat cheese.

FRIED GREEN TOMATOES WITH GOAT CHEESE BASIL GRITS

2 large green tomatoes

1 cup white cornmeal

½ cup all-purpose flour

1 teaspoon sweet paprika

1 teaspoon Lawry's Seasoned Salt

1 egg

⅓ cup milk

1 cup canola oil

Goat Cheese Basil Grits (recipe follows)

Core the tomatoes and slice off the ends so each end of the fruit is flat. Cut the tomatoes into 4 round slices each and set aside. In a small bowl, mix the cornmeal, flour, paprika, and seasoned salt. In a second bowl, whisk the egg and milk until thoroughly combined. Dredge each tomato slice in the seasoned flour mixture, then dip in the egg wash, and return to the flour mixture to cover.

In a cast-iron skillet or heavy sauté pan, heat the canola oil until bubbling. Place the breaded tomatoes in the pan and cook for about 2 minutes per side, or until golden brown. Transfer the tomatoes to paper towels to drain. Serve with the grits.

MAKES 4 SERVINGS

GOAT CHEESE BASIL GRITS

3 cups water

1 teaspoon sea salt

1¼ cups quick-cooking grits

1 tablespoon unsalted butter

2 tablespoons cream

4 ounces goat cheese

2 tablespoons chopped basil,
   for garnish

In a heavy saucepan, bring the water and salt to a boil over high heat. Stir in the grits and butter and bring back to a boil. Add the cream and decrease the heat to low, simmering for about 5 minutes, or until the mixture is creamy and thick. Remove the pan from the stove and whisk in the goat cheese until melted. Garnish with the basil.

MAKES 4 SERVINGS

Say Cheese

We're blessed to have a number of local creameries producing excellent artisanal cow cheeses from Yellow Branch Farm and superior farmstead goat cheeses from Three Graces, Looking Glass, and Spinning Spider. Our restaurant incorporates as much local goat cheese as we can in dishes such as our Goat Cheese Grits. The mountain elevation goes hand in hand with Old World cheese-making traditions and results in quality cheeses.

The pinto bean is generally considered everyman fare but paired with this tantalizing, fresh salsa, the humble legume is elevated to new heights. We serve this with a poached egg on top for breakfast as our own riff on huevos rancheros. Save the extra salsa for munching with chips down the road since it will keep nicely in the refrigerator for over 2 weeks.

SALSA VERDE PINTO BEANS

SALSA VERDE

MAKES 4 CUPS

1 large Vidalia onion, chopped

1 pound tomatillos, chopped

1 poblano pepper, seeded and chopped

1 jalapeño pepper, seeded and chopped

Juice of ½ lime

2 cloves garlic

1 tablespoon minced fresh cilantro

2 teaspoons ground cumin

1½ teaspoons sea salt

1½ teaspoons freshly ground black pepper

1½ teaspoons chili powder

1 tablespoon brown sugar

½ teaspoon oregano

¾ cup water

2 (14-ounce) cans pinto beans, drained

To make the salsa verde, combine the onion, tomatillos, poblano pepper, jalapeño pepper, lime juice, and garlic in a food processor and pulse until coarsely ground. Place the vegetable mixture, along with the cilantro, cumin, salt, pepper, chili powder, brown sugar, oregano, and water in a heavy saucepan and bring to a boil. Decrease the heat and simmer for 15 to 20 minutes, until the liquid is reduced by one-fourth.

Combine the pinto beans with 2 cups salsa verde and simmer for about 15 minutes, or until thick and saucy, before serving.

MAKES 6 TO 8 SERVINGS

Mountain Music

Asheville has a rich music history, beginning with the traditional Scotch-Irish tunes brought to the mountains by early settlers. Traditional mountain music of old English ballads eventually evolved into bluegrass and more recently "newgrass," a mixture of bluegrass and rock and roll. Today Asheville's lively music scene varies from nationally known singer/songwriters to indie rock to classical performances. The area is also host to a number of festivals featuring live music, including the Mountain Dance and Folk Festival, Bele Chere, Goombay, and LEAF.

We don't have stuffing in the South, unless you're referring to filling scarecrows with straw. We have dressing, which never sees the inside of a bird. We also tend to like dressing outside the holidays because it's just so good. This is a fantastic Thanksgiving or Christmas accompaniment, of course, but why limit your dressing intake to twice a year? Try this as a side to 'cue or char-grilled chicken.

CANDIED-GINGER CORNBREAD DRESSING

1 cup peeled and sliced fresh ginger (about 4 ounces ginger), or 1 (4-ounce) box crystallized ginger

1 cup water

½ cup sugar

8 tablespoons unsalted butter

2 large Vidalia onions, diced (about 8 cups)

2 cups thinly sliced celery (about 8 celery ribs)

8 ounces cremini mushrooms, quartered

1 teaspoon sea salt

1 teaspoon freshly ground black pepper

1 tablespoon minced sage

1 tablespoon minced fresh parsley

Buttery Cornbread (recipe follows, about 10 cups crumbled)

1 (14-ounce) can chicken stock

Bring the ginger, water, and sugar to a boil in a small saucepan over high heat. Boil until the water has evaporated and the ginger is caramelized. Remove from the heat and cool. Mince the candied ginger and set aside.

Preheat the oven to 325°F. Butter a 9 by 13-inch casserole. In a large skillet, melt 4 tablespoons of the butter over high heat and sauté the onions, celery, mushrooms, salt, and pepper for 5 to 7 minutes, until the onions are translucent and the celery is tender. Decrease the heat to low and stir in the remaining 4 tablespoons butter, the sage, and parsley, stirring until the butter is melted.

In a large bowl, crumble the cornbread and add the sautéed vegetables, ginger, and stock, mixing well. Place the dressing in the prepared casserole and bake uncovered for about 40 minutes, or until the top is crispy and the interior is moist but not soggy.

MAKES 8 TO 10 SERVINGS

This is the basis for our Candied Ginger Cornbread Dressing, but it's also the recipe we recommend using for your bread basket.

BUTTERY CORNBREAD

3½ cups yellow self-rising cornmeal

½ cup unsalted butter, melted

1½ cups whole milk

¼ cup heavy cream

3 eggs

Preheat the oven to 350°F. Butter a 9 by 13-inch glass baking dish. In a large bowl, combine the cornmeal, melted butter, milk, and heavy cream. In a separate bowl, beat the eggs and then add to the cornmeal mixture. Pour into the baking dish and bake for about 35 minutes, or until golden brown.

MAKES 8 TO 10 SERVINGS

BLUE RIDGE PARKWAY BRUNCHES

Pain Perdu with Cinnamon Sugar,
Blueberry Preserves, and Toasted Almonds

Tupelo Honey Ginormous Biscuits

Tomato Pie

Blueberry Granola Crunch Pancakes

Griddled Blackberry
Breakfast Bread Pudding

Broccoli and New Potato Quiche

Sweet Potato Pancakes with
Peach Butter and Spiced Pecans

Shiitake Sweet Potato Hash

Just the word *brunch* conjures up a free day, time off to do whatever the heck you feel like doing. We're blessed with a variety of leisure opportunities in our mountains, ranging from the ambitious (hiking, cycling, and paddling along the Blue Ridge Parkway) to the relaxed (strolling through art galleries, the gardens at the North Carolina Arboretum, or the shelves of Malaprop's bookstore) to the totally chilled (a nap in front of a roaring fire or forty winks on the front porch swing). Regardless of your activity on your day off, you'll need a certain amount of fortification, and these recipes will prepare you for whatever agenda you choose.

In Asheville, we believe you should always pursue the path that suits you best and, above all else, set out to tackle it on Asheville time, which is to say at your own pace, in your own style, and with a spirit free and unfettered. So, if you're an early riser, strike out on a walk or hike when the mountain air is brisk and the sun is just coming up, and then come back to your cozy kitchen and treat yourself to one of these dishes. Or, if your internal clock calls for a leisurely morning in your jammies, enjoy the specialness of drinking bloody marys and mimosas and preparing brunch for friends. Just remember the rule in our town is, you can do things anyway you like, so there's nothing to keep these brunch recipes from being supper recipes paired with a nice bottle of wine or your favorite microbrew. It's your day, your time, after all, so by all means, don't forget to serve yourself—routinely—a big heaping helping of carpe diem.

With a nod to the fertile cradle of fantastic food known as New Orleans, this take on French toast will become a favorite of breakfast eaters at your kitchen table. Be sure you use challah (braided egg bread). And if you've got some French Quarter coffee with chicory, bring it on.

PAIN PERDU WITH CINNAMON SUGAR, BLUEBERRY PRESERVES, AND TOASTED ALMONDS

½ cup sliced almonds

8 eggs

1¼ cups whole milk

4 tablespoons sugar

1 teaspoon vanilla extract

1½ teaspoons cinnamon

⅛ teaspoon nutmeg

Zest and juice of 1 lemon

1 loaf challah bread, cut into
    8 thick slices

1 tablespoon butter

1 tablespoon powdered sugar

Blueberry Preserves (page 37)

Preheat the oven to 350°F. Place the almonds on a rimmed sheet pan and bake for about 10 minutes, or until golden. Remove from the oven and allow to cool. Combine the eggs, milk, sugar, vanilla, ½ teaspoon of the cinnamon, and the nutmeg in a large bowl. Add the lemon zest and juice and stir thoroughly. This batter can be made in advance and refrigerated for up to 1 week.

Dip the bread slices into the batter, allowing the mixture to thoroughly absorb into the bread on both sides. Melt butter in a nonstick skillet over medium heat and cook the soaked challah for 4 to 5 minutes on each side, until golden brown. Mix together the powdered sugar and the remaining 1 teaspoon of cinnamon. Serve with the blueberry sauce and toasted almonds and sprinkle cinnamon sugar on top.

MAKES 4 SERVINGS

At Tupelo Honey Cafe, biscuits are omnipresent, in part because our guests love them, but also because they serve a utilitarian purpose: sopping. Sure they're great on their own with butter, jam, or honey, but don't forget the incredible sauces, juices, and gravies that deserve to be sopped by these delicious culinary worker bees.

TUPELO HONEY GINORMOUS BISCUITS

2 cups bread flour

1 tablespoon baking powder

¼ teaspoon baking soda

2 tablespoons sour cream

1 teaspoon plus ½ teaspoon salt

¾ cup unsalted butter, frozen

½ cup buttermilk

1 tablespoon butter, melted

Preheat the oven to 450°F. Combine the flour, baking powder, baking soda, sour cream, and ½ teaspoon of the salt in a large bowl. With a cheese grater, grate the frozen butter using the largest holes; quickly cut the butter into the flour mixture with a pastry cutter or fork until the mixture resembles coarse meal. Add the buttermilk to the flour mixture and stir just until combined. Do not overmix. On a floured surface, turn out the dough and roll out to a 1-inch thickness. Using a 3-inch biscuit cutter, cut the biscuits and place on a rimmed sheet pan. Cook on the top rack of the oven for about 20 minutes, or until light brown, and remove from the oven. Brush the melted butter on top of each biscuit and return to the oven for about 5 minutes longer, or until the biscuits are golden brown.

MAKES 6 BISCUITS

Can you say scrumptious? This decadent pie is at its amazing best during late summer, when the heirloom tomatoes in the mountains are at their juicy peak. (Chef Brian likes Brandywine or Cherokee purple tomatoes best.) You can also serve this for lunch or dinner with tossed salad greens and some crusty bread.

TOMATO PIE

Pie Dough (page 141)

2 cups shredded sharp cheddar cheese (about 10 ounces cheese)

1 cup mayonnaise

1½ tablespoons chopped fresh parsley

2 chopped green onions, white and green parts

1 tablespoon grated Parmesan cheese

1 cup panko bread crumbs

1½ pounds tomatoes, sliced ½ inch thick

Roll out a 10-inch pie crust and place in a 9-inch pie pan. Preheat the oven to 425°F. In a bowl, combine the cheddar cheese, mayonnaise, parsley, green onions, Parmesan cheese, and bread crumbs, mixing completely. Layer one-third of the tomatoes in the pie pan, covering the bottom of the pie crust. Spread one-third of the Parmesan cheese mixture on top of the tomatoes and repeat, making 2 more layers of tomatoes and cheese and ending with the cheese mixture. Bake for about 30 minutes, or until the top of the pie is bubbling and browned. Serve warm.

MAKES 8 SERVINGS

Our town is often called "crunchy," we believe, at least in part, with deference to the amount of granola we consume. We make our own granola at Tupelo Honey Cafe, and this recipe will convince you to do the same. Here, it's paired with buttermilk pancakes and dried blueberries, although you can use fresh or frozen blueberries as well.

BLUEBERRY GRANOLA CRUNCH PANCAKES

2¾ cups all-purpose flour

1 teaspoon sea salt

5 tablespoons plus
   1½ teaspoons sugar

1½ teaspoons baking soda

1 tablespoon baking powder

3 cups buttermilk

3 eggs

½ teaspoon cinnamon

⅛ teaspoon nutmeg

1 tablespoon tupelo honey

1 cup dried blueberries,
   reconstituted in warm water
   and drained

2 cups THC Granola
   (recipe follows)

2 tablespoons melted butter

Powdered sugar, for dusting

Combine the flour, salt, sugar, baking soda, and baking powder in a large bowl. In a medium bowl, whisk the buttermilk, eggs, cinnamon, nutmeg, and honey. Pour the liquid mixture into the flour mixture and blend well. Cook the pancakes over medium-high heat in a skillet or on a griddle, using about ½ cup batter per pancake, for about 3 minutes per side, or until brown on both sides. Top with the blueberries and granola and drizzle with the melted butter. Dust with a sprinkling of powdered sugar.

MAKES 6 TO 8 SERVINGS

THC GRANOLA

½ cup canola oil

1 cup pure maple syrup

2 teaspoons vanilla extract

6 cups old-fashioned rolled oats

1 cup shelled sunflower seeds
(about 4 ounces)

1½ cups sliced almonds (about
4 ounces)

1 tablespoon cinnamon

1 cup diced dried apples or
other dried fruit of your
choice (about 4 ounces dried
fruit)

½ cup coconut flakes, toasted

Preheat the oven to 300°F. In a small saucepan, combine the canola oil and maple syrup and bring to a boil. Add the vanilla. In a large bowl, combine the oats, sunflower seeds, almonds, cinnamon, and dried apples. Drizzle the syrup mixture over the dry ingredients, mixing well. Spread out the oats mixture on a rimmed sheet pan and bake for 30 to 40 minutes, until light brown. You'll know it's done by tasting the almonds: they should be toasted and not chewy. Remove the granola from the oven and cool. On another rimmed sheet pan, toast the coconut for about 5 minutes, or until just golden brown. Mix the coconut with the granola mixture. Store in an airtight container for up to 2 weeks.

Blackberries and blueberries are abundant in the mountains during the summertime, and this breakfast bread pudding is reason enough to venture out with a bucket and pick them. You can also substitute blueberries in this recipe if you prefer. Serve blueberry pudding with Blueberry Preserves (page 37) and blackberry pudding with Blackberry Skillet Jam (page 38).

GRIDDLED BLACKBERRY BREAKFAST BREAD PUDDING

6 eggs

1 cup heavy cream

¾ cup half-and-half

⅓ cup firmly packed brown sugar

½ cup granulated sugar

2 teaspoons ground nutmeg

1 teaspoon ground cinnamon

1 tablespoon vanilla extract

1 loaf challah bread, cut into 2-inch cubes

2½ cups fresh blackberries (about 1 pound)

8 ounces cream cheese, cubed

1 tablespoon butter

Blackberry Skillet Jam (page 38)

Preheat the oven to 325°F and butter a 6 by 12-inch casserole dish 4 inches deep. In a large bowl, combine the eggs, cream, half-and-half, brown sugar, granulated sugar, nutmeg, cinnamon, and vanilla and whisk until thoroughly blended. Add the bread cubes, blackberries, and cream cheese and combine with your hands until well mixed. Cover with foil and bake for about 1 hour, or until firm, then remove the foil and bake for 10 to 15 minutes longer, until the top browns. Remove from the oven, cool, and refrigerate overnight.

When ready to prepare the pudding, remove the set mixture from the casserole dish, and cut into 2-inch-thick slices. Melt the butter in a skillet over medium-high heat and brown the slices on both sides for 3 to 4 minutes on each side, until golden brown and hot all the way through. Serve with the jam.

MAKES 8 TO 10 SERVINGS

This cheesy quiche is heartier than some with its new potatoes and cream. It's reminiscent of a classic scalloped potato casserole with the addition of broccoli, all perched atop a flaky pie crust. This is also a winning addition to a chilly fall evening, a fireplace, and a glass of wine.

BROCCOLI AND NEW POTATO QUICHE

Pie Dough (page 141)

3 large red new potatoes

1 bunch broccoli (6 to 8 ounces), cut into small florets

2 teaspoons unsalted butter

½ large onion, diced

5 eggs

¾ cup heavy cream

1 teaspoon sea salt

1 teaspoon freshly ground black pepper

1 cup shredded sharp cheddar cheese (about 4 ounces)

Preheat the oven to 350°F. Roll out 2 (10-inch) pie crusts and place each one in a 9-inch pie pan. Crimp the edges of the pie crust with a fork and prick the bottom of the crust a couple of times. Bake for about 10 minutes, or until lightly browned.

Bring a medium saucepan of water to a boil, add the potatoes, and cook for about 15 minutes, or until the potatoes are tender, then transfer to an ice bath using a slotted spoon so you can reuse the cooking water. Add the broccoli to the boiling water and blanch for 2 minutes before transferring to the ice bath.

Melt the butter in a small skillet over medium heat and sauté the onion for 6 to 8 minutes, or until translucent. Set the onion aside. In a large bowl, beat the eggs and whisk in the cream, salt, and pepper. Remove the potatoes and broccoli from the ice bath and dry on paper towels. Dice the potatoes and set aside.

To build the quiche, begin with spreading ¼ cup of the cheese on the bottom of the crust and then layer the potatoes, broccoli, and onion. Cover the vegetables with the remaining cheese and pour the egg mixture evenly over the top. Place the pie pan on a rimmed sheet pan and bake for about 50 minutes, or until golden brown. Let rest for 5 minutes and serve immediately.

MAKES 2 PIES

The Great Outdoors

Asheville is recognized as a top destination for outdoor adventure lovers. With the magnificent natural beauty of the area, there are a multitude of ways to take it all in—from rafting and kayaking to horseback rides and llama trekking to mountain biking and hiking. Enjoy fly-fishing, hot-air ballooning, rock climbing, or a stroll through the North Carolina Arboretum and its expansive gardens and grounds.

This is our most requested recipe and one of our customers' favorites. It was also featured by Rachael Ray on the Food Network. As you know, the sweet potato is pretty revered in our mountains (and at Tupelo Honey Cafe), so the idea of turning this vitamin-packed vegetable into breakfast is ingenious. The result is a pancake that has a hint of cinnamon and nutmeg but the warm character of the spud it praises. Serve these with a side of hickory-smoked bacon.

SWEET POTATO PANCAKES WITH PEACH BUTTER AND SPICED PECANS

1 large sweet potato

2¾ cups all-purpose flour

1 teaspoon salt

5 tablespoons plus
    1½ teaspoons sugar

¾ teaspoon baking soda

1½ teaspoons baking powder

3 cups buttermilk

3 eggs

2 tablespoons unsalted butter,
    melted

2 tablespoons tupelo honey

1 teaspoon cinnamon

½ teaspoon nutmeg

Peach Butter (page 40)

Spiced Pecans (recipe follows)

Wrap the sweet potato in foil and bake in a 350°F oven for about 45 minutes, or until tender. Set aside to cool to room temperature. In a large bowl, combine the flour, salt, sugar, baking soda, and baking powder. In another large bowl, whisk together the buttermilk, eggs, and melted butter. Add the wet mixture to the dry mixture. Peel the cooled sweet potato, place in a medium bowl, and mash. Add the honey, cinnamon, and nutmeg and mix well. Add the sweet potato mixture to the pancake batter, combining well, and let the batter stand for 1 hour. Heat a skillet over medium heat and ladle the batter in batches, ⅓ cup at a time, cooking the pancakes until browned on each side. Serve with the peach butter and spiced pecans.

MAKES 4 SERVINGS

SPICED PECANS

1½ teaspoons tupelo honey

¼ teaspoon cayenne pepper

¼ teaspoon sea salt

1½ teaspoons unsalted butter

1 cup chopped pecans

In a bowl, mix the honey, cayenne, and salt. Melt the butter in a skillet over medium heat. Add the honey mixture and the pecans and cook for 8 to 10 minutes, until lightly browned and caramelized. Remove from the heat, cool, and store in an airtight container.

MAKES 1 CUP

The Blue Ridge Parkway

The Blue Ridge Parkway is a 469-mile scenic byway following the spine of the Appalachian Mountains through Virginia and North Carolina. It runs through Asheville, where the parkway's headquarters and welcome center are located, and provides area residents and visitors with a beautiful motoring road into the mountains. Cyclists and hikers are active on the parkway as well.

While this savory hash is delicious with eggs (served any way you like them), we also love this dish with roasted duck breast or duck confit, since its earthy flavor plays off the richness of duck. The southern Appalachian region is conducive to mushroom cultivation, and many farmers are now growing their own shiitakes.

SHIITAKE SWEET POTATO HASH

4 cups water

1 large sweet potato, peeled and diced

2 tablespoons olive oil

1 pound shiitake mushrooms, stems removed and discarded, caps thinly sliced

¼ cup sliced green onions, white and green parts

2 teaspoons minced fresh sage

1 teaspoon hot pepper sauce

2 tablespoons tupelo honey

⅛ teaspoon sea salt

⅛ teaspoon freshly ground black pepper

Bring the water to a boil in a heavy saucepan. Add the sweet potato and blanch for about 5 minutes, or until the potatoes are just fork tender. Remove the potatoes and transfer to an ice bath. Heat 1 tablespoon of the olive oil in a heavy skillet over medium-high heat and sauté the mushrooms for 3 to 4 minutes, until just tender, and set aside.

In a large bowl, combine the sweet potato, mushrooms, green onions, sage, hot pepper sauce, honey, salt, and pepper. In a nonstick skillet, heat the remaining 1 tablespoon of olive oil over high heat and add the potato mixture. Sauté for 8 to 10 minutes, until the mixture is caramelized. Serve immediately.

MAKES 4 SERVINGS

AS SWEET AS TUPELO HONEY

Mocha Cheesecake

Chocolate Pecan Pie

Banana Pudding

Maple Sweet Potato Pudding

Candied-Ginger Crème Brûlée

Three-Berry Cream Cheese Pie

Peach Cobbler with Candied Almonds

For some folks, dessert is show-off time. As in, "I just whipped this up this afternoon" or "I just threw this together at the last minute" as you bring out some zillion-layered cake or intensely rich pie, or flaming thing-a-ma-jig. Balderdash, we say. Dessert should be the crowning dining moment all right, but it doesn't have to cause you to experience kitchen panic as you watch your chocolate soufflé fall. Our desserts at Tupelo Honey are honest and unfussy, but no less delicious or satisfying than one of those desserts you have to order an hour before you expect to eat it. We bring vegetables and fruits to our dessert roster, too, believing some of the best ideas involve taking something already delicious and making it even delicious-er with the introduction of ingredients such as butter, sugar, honey, maple syrup, ginger, cinnamon, and chocolate.

Sure, some of our end-of-meal offerings are pretty rich. You just have to pace yourself. Take a break from the table and serve dessert and coffee in the living room. Or heck, have dessert first. Our point is, it should be pure pleasure, simple indulgence, the fond farewell at the end of an extraordinary dinner with family and friends. It should be tempting, but not painful. Worth it, without a trace of guilt. Sweet, and full of amazing flavors. Remember Erma Bombeck's sentiment: "Think, after all, of all those women on-board the *Titanic* who passed on the dessert tray." Don't pass on these memorable endings.

"I have no idea why I've always been so in love with southern food. If I were Shirley MacLaine, I'd swear that I'd been southern in an earlier life."

—Jean Anderson, *A Love Affair with Southern Cooking*

Who doesn't love the decadence of cheesecake, especially one that brings the tannic depth of dark chocolate and coffee to a fevered pitch? This recipe takes some time, mainly time spent waiting for it to be completely done and ready to serve. But trust us, it is worth every minute. The cheesecake needs to be refrigerated overnight before serving.

MOCHA CHEESECAKE

1½ cups ground graham crackers (about 15 crackers)

4 tablespoons unsalted butter, melted

2 cups strong coffee

2 teaspoons cornstarch

2 teaspoons water

1½ cups bittersweet dark chocolate chips (about 8 ounces)

2 cups sugar

1 teaspoon sea salt

3 (8-ounce) packages cream cheese

8 eggs

Preheat the oven to 300°F and line the bottom of a 10-inch springform pan with aluminum foil. Rub room temperature butter around the edges of the bottom of the pan. Combine the graham cracker crumbs and melted butter in a small bowl and press the mixture into the bottom of the pan.

Simmer the coffee in a saucepan over low heat until reduced to 1 cup. Combine the cornstarch and water in a small bowl and stir into the hot coffee. Add the chocolate, sugar, and salt to the coffee mixture and stir until the chocolate is melted and the mixture is thoroughly blended. Remove from the heat and set aside. In a food processor, combine the cream cheese and coffee mixture, blending until smooth. With the processor running, add the eggs, one at a time, until well blended. Pour the cheesecake mixture into the prepared pan and place onto a rimmed sheet pan.

Place the pan on the oven's top rack and bake for 1½ hours, then reduce the heat to 200°F and cook for about 30 minutes longer, or until the cheesecake is set and firm. Leaving the oven door closed, turn off the heat and leave the cheesecake in the oven for 10 minutes more. Take the cheesecake out of the oven and cool at room temperature for 30 minutes. Refrigerate overnight before serving.

MAKES 1 (10-INCH) CAKE; 12 SERVINGS

As Sweet as Tupelo Honey

CHOCOLATE PECAN PIE

Pie Dough (page 141)

¾ cup light corn syrup

¾ cup sugar

⅛ teaspoon sea salt

3 eggs

1 teaspoon vanilla extract

3 tablespoons tupelo honey

½ cup unsalted butter, melted

1½ cups pecan pieces (about 6 ounces)

½ cup semisweet chocolate chips

Roll out 1 (11-inch) pie crust, lay it in a 10-inch pie pan, and crimp the edges. Preheat the oven to 350°F. In a large bowl, combine the corn syrup, sugar, salt, eggs, vanilla, and honey, mixing well. Stir in the melted butter. Pour the mixture into the pie crust. Top with the pecans and chocolate chips. Bake the pie, rotating halfway through cooking, for about 1 hour and 15 minutes, or until the crust is brown and the pie filling is bubbly. Serve this pie warm with vanilla ice cream or sweetened whipped cream.

MAKES 1 (10-INCH) PIE

Nothing is more comforting or reminiscent of a happy home than banana pudding. It's as American as, well, apple pie but brings the sweet and sunny yellowness of bananas and vanilla wafers to the forefront. The pudding needs to be refrigerated overnight before serving.

BANANA PUDDING

3 cups whole milk

2 egg yolks

¾ cup sugar

4 tablespoons cornstarch

¼ teaspoon sea salt

2 teaspoons vanilla extract

2 tablespoons unsalted butter

3 ripe bananas

24 vanilla wafers

Sweetened whipped cream,
   for serving

In a heavy saucepan, place the milk over medium heat until it begins to simmer, then turn the heat down to low. In a small bowl, combine the egg yolks, sugar, cornstarch, salt, and vanilla until the mixture is creamy. With a teaspoon, add a little of the warm milk to the egg yolks to ensure the yolks don't curdle. Then add the yolk mixture to the pan of warm milk, stirring over low heat for 5 to 6 minutes, until the mixture thickens and coats the back of a spoon. Stir in the butter until melted and remove the mixture from the heat. Slicing as you go, cover the bottom of a casserole dish with the bananas. Pour the pudding mixture over the bananas and top with the vanilla wafers. Refrigerate overnight before serving with a dollop of whipped cream.

MAKES 6 SERVINGS

This is a fantastic fall and holiday dessert that offers a change of pace from your expected pumpkin pie. It is also another Tupelo Honey love sonnet to the diversity and flavor of the much revered sweet potato. The pudding should be refrigerated overnight before serving.

MAPLE SWEET POTATO
PUDDING

2 small sweet potatoes

2 cups whole milk

⅔ cup pure maple syrup

2 egg yolks

2 tablespoons sugar

2 tablespoons cornstarch

½ teaspoon vanilla extract

½ teaspoon cinnamon

2 tablespoons brown sugar

½ teaspoon sea salt

2 tablespoons unsalted butter

Sweetened whipped cream,
    for serving

Wrap the sweet potatoes in foil and bake in a 350°F oven for about 45 minutes, or until tender. Set aside. Heat the milk and maple syrup in a heavy saucepan over medium heat until it reaches a simmer, then reduce the heat to low. In a small bowl, cream together the egg yolks, sugar, and cornstarch. Place a teaspoon of the warm milk mixture in the egg yolks, stirring to prevent the yolks from curdling. Add the yolk mixture to the warm milk and then add the vanilla and cinnamon, continuing to cook for about 5 minutes, or until the mixture thickens and coats the back of a spoon. Peel the sweet potatoes and put the soft flesh in a medium bowl. Add the brown sugar, salt, and butter and blend until smooth. Whisk the potato mixture into the warm milk mixture until well combined. Pour the pudding into a casserole and cool at room temperature for 30 minutes before refrigerating overnight. Serve with whipped cream.

MAKES 8 SERVINGS

The candied ginger in this classic dessert adds a sweet spiciness to the rich custard. It's a delicious holiday dessert with roast turkey or ham and Candied Ginger Cornbread Dressing. Don't let the water bath technique trip you up—it's easy! The custards need to be refrigerated overnight before serving.

CANDIED GINGER
CRÈME BRÛLÉE

8 cups heavy cream

2 tablespoons vanilla extract

¾ cup sugar

1 cup or approximately 16 extra
   large egg yolks

⅛ teaspoon sea salt

6 tablespoons minced candied
   ginger (page 182) or
   purchased crystallized
   ginger

6 ounces brown sugar

Preheat the oven to 300°F. Place 8 (8-ounce) ramekins or soufflé cups in a baking pan. Heat the cream and vanilla in a heavy saucepan over medium heat until the mixture begins to simmer. In a medium bowl, combine the sugar, egg yolks, and salt. Spoon 2 tablespoons of the hot cream mixture into the egg mixture to prevent the eggs from curdling. Add the egg mixture to the hot cream and simmer for about 5 minutes, or until the mixture coats the back of a spoon. Place 2 teaspoons of the candied ginger in each ramekin. Top the ginger with the cream mixture until the cups are almost full. Add water to the pan so that it covers the ramekins halfway. Bake for about 1 hour, or until lightly browned. Remove the ramekins from the water bath, cool to room temperature, and refrigerate overnight. To serve, sprinkle each custard with 1 tablespoon of the brown sugar and place under the broiler until the sugar caramelizes. You can also caramelize the sugar using a kitchen butane torch, if you have one.

MAKES 8 SERVINGS

This is a fruity (and somewhat sneaky) cousin to the cheesecake, topped with the bountiful berries we have in our mountains (you can also use frozen berries). It's quicker than the standard cheesecake recipe, and we think it's equally scrumptious. The pie needs to be refrigerated overnight before serving.

THREE-BERRY
CREAM CHEESE PIE

1½ cups ground vanilla wafers (40 wafers)

4 tablespoons unsalted butter, melted

1 cup blueberries, fresh or frozen

1 cup blackberries, fresh or frozen

1 cup raspberries, fresh or frozen

½ cup plus 2 tablespoons sugar

1 tablespoon water

1 tablespoon cornstarch

2 (8-ounce) packages softened cream cheese

2 eggs

1 tablespoon vanilla extract

⅛ teaspoon sea salt

2 tablespoons heavy cream

Preheat the oven to 400°F and lightly butter a 9-inch deep-dish pie dish. In a medium bowl, combine the vanilla wafers and melted butter and press the mixture into the baking dish, evenly covering the bottom and sides, and set aside. Combine the blueberries, blackberries, raspberries, and 2 tablespoons of the sugar in a heavy saucepan. And place over high heat for 5 to 6 minutes, until the mixture is a thick sauce (if you use fresh berries, reduce the cooking time to 3 minutes). Combine the water and cornstarch and add the mixture to the berries, cooking for about 2 minutes longer, or until the mixture thickens slightly. Set the berry mixture aside. Combine the cream cheese, the remaining ½ cup sugar, the eggs, vanilla, salt, and cream in a food processor until fluffy, using a spatula to scrap the sides of the processor until all the ingredients are thoroughly blended. Pour the cream mixture into the wafer crust and then pour the berry mixture on top of the cream filling. Bake for about 20 minutes, or until the pie is firm. Cool at room temperature for 30 minutes. Refrigerate overnight before serving.

MAKES 8 SERVINGS

Honey

While tupelo honey comes from special swamplands in Florida, western North Carolina produces an amazing amount of native honeys of all kinds. One of the most prized is sourwood honey, but it's a fun exercise to do a honey tasting and teach your palate to be discerning about the different nuances of buckwheat honey, blackberry honey, locust honey, and wildflower honey.

This is best when peaches are in season, but if you can't wait, you can substitute 2 (15-ounce) cans of peach halves. Drain and add back ½ cup of the syrup to the peaches. Adding vanilla ice cream on top is mandatory. No questions asked.

PEACH COBBLER WITH CANDIED ALMONDS

¾ cup plus ½ cup water

1 cup sugar

8 peaches, peeled, pitted, and quartered

2 teaspoons vanilla extract

1½ teaspoons cinnamon

1 cup blanched sliced almonds

2 tablespoons brown sugar

1 tablespoon cornstarch

¼ teaspoon nutmeg

⅛ teaspoon sea salt

Preheat the oven to 300°F. In a large bowl, combine ¾ cup of the water and ½ cup of the sugar, mixing until well combined, then add the peaches. Place the peaches in a covered baking dish and cook for 10 to 12 minutes, until bubbly, and set aside. Increase the oven temperature to 400°F. In a large bowl, combine the vanilla, the remaining ½ cup water, and 1 teaspoon of the cinnamon and then add the almonds, stirring well. Heat the almond mixture in a heavy skillet over high heat until it reaches a simmer and cook for about 4 minutes, or until the liquid is reduced by half. Spread the almonds onto a rimmed sheet pan and roast, stirring frequently, for about 7 minutes, or until the moisture is almost gone. Set the almonds aside to cool.

Drain the peaches, saving the syrup. Arrange the peaches in a 4-cup baking dish. Combine the reserved syrup, brown sugar, cornstarch, the remaining ½ teaspoon cinnamon, the nutmeg, and salt and pour over the peaches. Bake for about 20 minutes, or until golden brown. Top with the candied almonds and return to the oven for 3 to 5 minutes longer, or until the almonds are browned.

MAKES 6 TO 8 SERVINGS

RESOURCES

www.asap.org

www.bentonshams.com

www.hickorynutgap.com

www.southernfoodways.com

www.exploreasheville.com

www.air.com

www.spinningspidercreamery.com

www.threegraces.com

www.boiledpeanuts.com

www.ansonmills.com

www.flyingcloudfarm.net

www.sunbursttrout.com

www.yellowbranch.com

www.imaldris.com

METRIC CONVERSIONS AND EQUIVALENTS

APPROXIMATE METRIC EQUIVALENTS

Volume		Weight	
¼ teaspoon	1 milliliter	¼ ounce	7 grams
½ teaspoon	2.5 milliliters	½ ounce	14 grams
¾ teaspoon	4 milliliters	¾ ounce	21 grams
1 teaspoon	5 milliliters	1 ounce	28 grams
1¼ teaspoons	6 milliliters	1¼ ounces	35 grams
1½ teaspoons	7.5 milliliters	1½ ounces	42.5 grams
1¾ teaspoons	8.5 milliliters	1⅔ ounces	45 grams
2 teaspoons	10 milliliters	2 ounces	57 grams
1 tablespoon (½ fluid ounce)	15 milliliters	3 ounces	85 grams
2 tablespoons (1 fluid ounce)	30 milliliters	4 ounces (¼ pound)	113 grams
¼ cup	60 milliliters	5 ounces	142 grams
⅓ cup	80 milliliters	6 ounces	170 grams
½ cup (4 fluid ounces)	120 milliliters	7 ounces	198 grams
⅔ cup	160 milliliters	8 ounces (½ pound)	227 grams
¾ cup	180 milliliters	16 ounces (1 pound)	454 grams
1 cup (8 fluid ounces)	240 milliliters	35.25 ounces (2.2 pounds)	1 kilogram
1¼ cups	300 milliliters		
1½ cups (12 fluid ounces)	360 milliliters		
1⅔ cups	400 milliliters		
2 cups (1 pint)	460 milliliters		
3 cups	700 milliliters		
4 cups (1 quart)	0.95 liter		
1 quart plus ¼ cup	1 liter		
4 quarts (1 gallon)	3.8 liters		

Length

⅛ inch	3 millimeters	2½ inches	6 centimeters
¼ inch	6 millimeters	4 inches	10 centimeters
½ inch	1¼ centimeters	5 inches	13 centimeters
1 inch	2½ centimeters	6 inches	15¼ centimeters
2 inches	5 centimeters	12 inches (1 foot)	30 centimeters

COMMON INGREDIENTS AND THEIR APPROXIMATE EQUIVALENTS

1 cup uncooked white rice = 185 grams

1 cup all-purpose flour = 140 grams

1 stick butter (4 ounces • ½ cup • 8 tablespoons) = 110 grams

1 cup butter (8 ounces • 2 sticks • 16 tablespoons) = 220 grams

1 cup brown sugar, firmly packed = 225 grams

1 cup granulated sugar = 200 grams

METRIC CONVERSION FORMULAS

To Convert	Multiply
Ounces to grams	Ounces by 28.35
Pounds to kilograms	Pounds by .454
Teaspoons to milliliters	Teaspoons by 4.93
Tablespoons to milliliters	Tablespoons by 14.79
Fluid ounces to milliliters	Fluid ounces by 29.57
Cups to milliliters	Cups by 236.59
Cups to liters	Cups by .236
Pints to liters	Pints by .473
Quarts to liters	Quarts by .946
Gallons to liters	Gallons by 3.785
Inches to centimeters	Inches by 2.54

OVEN TEMPERATURES

To convert Fahrenheit to Celsius, subtract 32 from Fahrenheit, multiply the result by 5, then divide by 9.

Description	Fahrenheit	Celsius	British Gas Mark
Very cool	200°	95°	0
Very cool	225°	110°	¼
Very cool	250°	120°	½
Cool	275°	135°	1
Cool	300°	150°	2
Warm	325°	165°	3
Moderate	350°	175°	4
Moderately hot	375°	190°	5
Fairly hot	400°	200°	6
Hot	425°	220°	7
Very hot	450°	230°	8
Very hot	475°	245°	9

Information compiled from a variety of sources, including *Recipes into Type* by Joan Whitman and Dolores Simon (Newton, MA: Biscuit Books, 2000); *The New Food Lover's Companion* by Sharon Tyler Herbst (Hauppauge, NY: Barron's, 1995); and *Rosemary Brown's Big Kitchen Instruction Book* (Kansas City, MO: Andrews McMeel, 1998).

INDEX

A

Ager, Jamie, 151
AIR. *See* Asheville Independent Restaurant
    Association
Albers, Joseph, 73
Almond-Crusted Trout with Blackened
    Crawfish and Roasted Red Pepper
    Butter, 112–13
almonds, 91, 112–13, 187, 192, 215
Anderson, Jean, 201
Andouille Sausage Ragout, 158
Appalachian Sustainable Agriculture
    Project (ASAP), 124, 129
appetizers, 44, 45
    Baked Goat Cheese and Smoked Tomato
        Dip with Garlic Crostini, 51
    Cheesy Grits Cakes with Sunshot Salsa
        and Smoked Jalapeño Sauce, 60
    Crispy Fried Artichokes with Oven-
        Roasted Tomatoes and Lemon
        Vinaigrette, 47
    Mushroom Quesadilla with Green Tomato
        Salsa and Smoked Jalapeño Sauce,
        56–57
    Nut-Crusted Brie with Cabernet
        Balsamic–Glazed Figs, 52
    Tupelo Honey Wings, 58
    Warm Pimento Cheese and Chips, 55
apple harvest, 4
Apple Salsa, 4
apples
    Apple Salsa, 4
    Cherry Apple Chowchow, 39
    Chicken Apple Meat Loaf with Tarragon
        Tomato Gravy, 132–33
    dried, for Granola, 193
    Nut-Crusted Brie with Cabernet
        Balsamic–Glazed Figs, 52
Art Deco, 80
artichokes, Crispy Fried Artichokes with
    Oven-Roasted Tomatoes and Lemon
    Vinaigrette, 47
ASAP. *See* Appalachian Sustainable
    Agriculture Project
Asheville, North Carolina, xi, xiii–xv, xvii, 5,
    44, 70, 98, 145, 160, 197
Asheville City Market, 160
Asheville Independent Restaurant
    Association (AIR), 59
asparagus, Benne-Coated Asparagus, 167

B

bacon
    Bacony Egg Salad, 87
    Beef Tenderloin Wrapped in Maple-
        Peppered Bacon with Gorgonzola
        Gratinée and Green Peppercorn
        Bordelaise Sauce, 152
    Corn and Crab Chowder, 67
    Creamy Red-Eye Gravy, 12
    Low Country Gravy, 17
    Southern Fried Chicken BLT, 83
    Spinach Salad with Roasted Beets, Goat
        Cheese, Peppered Bacon, and Garlic
        Ranch Dressing, 90
Baked Goat Cheese and Smoked Tomato
    Dip with Garlic Crostini, 51
Balsamic-Glazed Figs, 53
banana, 73, 208
banana pepper, Roasted Corn Salsa, 6
Banana Pudding, 208
Basic Barbecue Sauce, 21
basil, fresh, 20, 27, 33, 48, 51, 79, 80,
    91, 103, 111, 136–37, 178
Basil Cashew Pesto, 33
Basil Cream Sauce, 103
Basil Roasted Red Pepper Mayonnaise, 80
Basil Vinaigrette, 27
beef
    Beef Tenderloin Wrapped in Maple-
        Peppered Bacon with Gorgonzola
        Gratinée and Green Peppercorn
        Bordelaise Sauce, 152
    Reuben with Chowchow, Swiss Cheese,
        and Thousand Island Dressing, 74
    Smoked Jalapeño–Glazed New York Strip
        Steak with Tomato Shallot Gravy, 159
Beef Tenderloin Wrapped in Maple-
    Peppered Bacon with Gorgonzola
    Gratinée and Green Peppercorn
    Bordelaise Sauce, 152
beer and wine pairings, xvii
beets
    Beets My Heart, 174
    Spinach Salad with Roasted Beets, Goat
        Cheese, Peppered Bacon, and Garlic
        Ranch Dressing, 90
    Tupelo Honey Pickled Beet Salad, 169
Beets My Heart, 174
Bele Chere, 181
Benne-Coated Asparagus, 167
bicolored corn, 6
Biltmore House, 44, 98, 106, 107
Black Mountain College, 70, 73
blackberries
    Blackberry Skillet Jam, 38
    Griddled Blackberry Breakfast Bread
        Pudding, 195
    Three-Berry Cream Cheese Pie, 212
Blackberry Skillet Jam, 38
Blackened Catfish with Sunshot Salsa, 109
Blackened Chicken Potpie, 138–39
Blackening Spice, 141
Blount, Roy, Jr., 2, 77, 99, 103

Blue Ridge Parkway, xv, 186, 200
blueberries
    dried, 153, 192
    fresh, 37, 187, 212
Blueberry Granola Crunch Pancakes, 192
Blueberry Preserves, 37
bluegrass music, xvii, 70
bok choy, 94
Bombeck, Erma, 204
Brandywine tomatoes, 8
Brewgrass Festival, xvii
Brie wheels, 52, 71
Broccoli and New Potato Quiche, 196
Bronzed Wild Sockeye Salmon with Roasted
    Corn Salsa, 120
brunch
    Blueberry Granola Crunch Pancakes, 192
    Broccoli and New Potato Quiche, 196
    Griddled Blackberry Breakfast Bread
        Pudding, 195
    Pain Perdu with Cinnamon Sugar,
        Blueberry Preserves, and Toasted
        Almonds, 187
    Shiitake Sweet Potato Hash, 201
    Sweet Potato Pancakes with Peach
        Butter and Spiced Pecans, 199–200
    Tomato Pie, 190
    Tupelo Honey Ginormous Biscuits, 189
buttermilk
    Blueberry Granola Crunch Pancakes, 192
    Buttermilk Pork Chops with Creamy Red-
        Eye Gravy, 146
    Garlic Ranch Dressing, 29
    Nutty Fried Chicken with Smashed Sweet
        Potatoes and Milk Gravy, 127
    Southern Fried Chicken BLT, 83
    Southern Fried Chicken Breasts with
        Cremini Sweet Onion Gravy, 125
    Sweet Potato Pancakes with Peach
        Butter and Spiced Pecans, 199–200
    Tupelo Honey Ginormous Biscuits, 189
Buttermilk Pork Chops with Creamy Red-
    Eye Gravy, 146
Buttery Cornbread, 183
Buttery Cracker-Baked Oysters with
    Rémoulade, 119

C

cabbage, 39, 93
Cage, John, 70, 73
Candied Ginger Crème Brûlée, 211
Candied-Ginger Cornbread Dressing, 182
Carolina Fish Chowder, 65
carrots, 18, 65, 81, 93, 94, 136–37,
    138–39, 158
    Lamb and Root Vegetable Stew Topped
        with Grits Croutons, 162–63

Tupelo Honey–Glazed Carrots, 177
cauliflower, Cheesy Mashed Cauliflower, 175
celery, 18, 65, 67, 81, 134, 136–37, 138–39, 150
Char-Grilled Pork Tenderloin with Peach Fennel Salsa, 155
Char-Grilled Swordfish with Marinated Green Tomatoes and Rosemary Aioli, 110
cheddar cheese
    Broccoli and New Potato Quiche, 196
    Cheesy Grits Cakes with Sunshot Salsa and Smoked Jalapeño Sauce, 60
    Cheesy Mashed Cauliflower, 175
    Cheesy Onion Bisque, 63
    Mushroom Quesadilla with Green Tomato Salsa and Smoked Jalapeño Sauce, 56–57
    Tomato Pie, 190
    Warm Pimento Cheese and Chips, 55
cheesecake
    Mocha Cheesecake, 205
    Three-Berry Cream Cheese Pie, 212
Cheesy Grits Cakes with Sunshot Salsa and Smoked Jalapeño Sauce, 60
Cheesy Mashed Cauliflower, 175
Cheesy Onion Bisque, 63
Cherokee Purple tomatoes, 8
cherries, dried, 18, 39
Cherry Apple Chowchow, 39
Cherry Truffle Gravy, 18
chicken, 124
    Blackened Chicken Potpie, 138–39
    Chicken Andouille Stir-Fry with Orange Jalapeño Glaze, 134
    Chicken Apple Meat Loaf with Tarragon Tomato Gravy, 132–33
    Herb-Roasted Whole Chicken with Savory Pan Gravy, 136–37
    Nutty Fried Chicken with Smashed Sweet Potatoes and Milk Gravy, 127
    Peachy Grilled Chicken Salad with Pecan Vinaigrette, 89
    Southern Chicken Saltimbocca with Country Ham in a Mushroom Marsala Sauce, 130–31
    Southern Fried Chicken BLT, 83
    Southern Fried Chicken Breasts with Cremini Sweet Onion Gravy, 125
    Tupelo Honey Chicken Sandwich with Havarti Cheese and Cranberry Mayonnaise, 76
    Tupelo Honey Wings, 58
Chicken Andouille Stir-Fry with Orange Jalapeño Glaze, 134
Chicken Apple Meat Loaf with Tarragon Tomato Gravy, 132–33
chocolate
    Chocolate Pecan Pie, 207
    Mocha Cheesecake, 205

Chocolate Pecan Pie, 207
Chorizo-Baked Sea Scallops with Basil Cream Sauce, 103
cilantro, fresh, 7, 23, 28, 81, 82, 180
Cilantro Lime Mayonnaise, 82
Claiborne, Craig, 101
coconut milk
    Blackened Chicken Potpie, 138–39
    Coconut Sweet Potato Bisque, 66
Coconut Sweet Potato Bisque, 66
coffee, 12
Coffee Molasses Barbecue Sauce, 24
corn, 6, 67
Corn and Crab Chowder, 67
cornbread, Buttery Cornbread, 182, 183
crabmeat, Corn and Crab Chowder, 67
Cranberry Mayonnaise, 34
Creamy Maple Mustard Dressing, 32
Creamy Red-Eye Gravy, 12
Creamy Tomato Soup, 62
Cremini Sweet Onion Gravy, 13
Creole Spice, 102
Crispy Fried Artichokes with Oven-Roasted Tomatoes and Lemon Vinaigrette, 47
Cunningham, Merce, 70, 73
Curry-Spiced Halibut with Chard and Oven-Roasted Tomatoes in Lemon Beurre Blanc, 116–17

D
de Kooning, Willem, 70, 73
Demi-Glace, 13
desserts
    Banana Pudding, 208
    Candied Ginger Crème Brulée, 211
    Chocolate Pecan Pie, 207
    Maple Sweet Potato Pudding, 209
    Mocha Cheesecake, 205
    Peach Cobbler with Candied Almonds, 215
    Three-Berry Cream Cheese Pie, 212
Dijonnaise, 85
Disney, Walt, 98
dressings and spreads, 26
    Basil Cashew Pesto, 33
    Basil Vinaigrette, 27
    Cranberry Mayonnaise, 34
    Creamy Maple Mustard Dressing, 32
    Garlic Ranch Dressing, 29
    Pecan Vinaigrette, 31
    Raspberry Honey Mayonnaise, 34
    Smoked Jalapeño Aiolo, 35
    Spicy Smoked Tomato Vinaigrette, 28
Duke's mayonnaise, 32, 55

E
Edge, John T., 2
Egerton, John, 166
Einstein, Albert, 73
Ellington, Douglas, 80

F
farmer's markets, 5, 145, 160
fennel, 5, 155
figs, 53
fish and seafood, 98
    Almond-Crusted Trout with Blackened Crawfish and Roasted Red Pepper Butter, 112–13
    Blackened Catfish with Sunshot Salsa, 109
    Bronzed Wild Sockeye Salmon with Roasted Corn Salsa, 120
    Buttery Cracker-Baked Oysters with Rémoulade, 119
    Carolina Fish Chowder, 65
    Char-Grilled Swordfish with Marinated Green Tomatoes and Rosemary Aioli, 110
    Chorizo-Baked Sea Scallops with Basil Cream Sauce, 103
    Curry-Spiced Halibut with Chard and Oven-Roasted Tomatoes in Lemon Beurre Blanc, 116–17
    Pecan-Crusted Red Snapper with Spiced Black Beans and Orange Cilantro Butter, 114
    Shrimp and Goat Cheese Grits with Roasted Red Pepper Sauce, 101
    Smoked Salmon–Wrapped Sea Scallops with Capers and Pickled Onion Aioli, 121
    Spice-Crusted Tuna with Seared Crab Cakes and Lemon Hollandaise, 104
Fit for the King Peanut Butter and Banana Sandwich, 73
Fitzgerald, F. Scott, xiv, 104
Flying Cloud Farm, 151
food memories, xi
Foodtopian society, xiv–xv
The French Broad Brewing Company, xv
French toast, 187
Fried Green Tomato and Grilled Portobello Sandwich with Basil Roasted Red Pepper Mayonnaise, 79
Fried Green Tomatoes with Goat Cheese Basil Grits, 178
Fuller, Buckminster, xiv, 70, 73

G
Garlic Crostini, 51
Garlic Ranch Dressing, 29
garlic, roasted oil or puree, 5
ginger, candied or crystallized, 211
ginger, fresh, 77, 86, 182
goat cheese, 51, 79, 90, 94, 101, 178, 179
Goat Cheese Basil Grits, 179
Goombay, 181
granola, THC Granola, 193
Grateful Dead Black Bean Burger with Cilantro Lime Mayonnaise, 81

gravies and sauces, 9
    Basic Barbecue Sauce, 21
    Cherry Truffle Gravy, 18
    Coffee Molasses Barbecue Sauce, 24
    Creamy Red-Eye Gravy, 12
    Cremini Sweet Onion Gravy, 13
    Low Country Gravy, 17
    Milk Gravy, 10
    Orange Cilantro Gravy, 19
    Root Beer–Sorghum Molasses Glaze, 24
    Sausage Gravy, 10
    Smoked Jalapeño Sauce, 23
    Smoked Tomato Sauce, 20
    Tarragon Tomato Gravy, 133
    Tomato Shallot Gravy, 16
    Tupelo Honey Wing Sauce, 22
Green Man, xv
green peppercorns, 152
green tomato
    Fried Green Tomato and Grilled
        Portobello Sandwich with Basil
        Roasted Red Pepper Mayonnaise, 79
    Fried Green Tomatoes with Goat Cheese
        Basil Grits, 178
    Green Tomato Salsa, 7
    Marinated Green Tomatoes, 111
    Pickled Green Tomato Salad with Fresh
        Mozzarella, 86
Green Tomato Salsa, 7
Griddled Blackberry Breakfast Bread
    Pudding, 195
Grilled Club Sandwich with Brie and
    Raspberry Honey Mayonnaise, 71
grits, 99
    Cheesy Grits Cakes with Sunshot Salsa
        and Smoked Jalapeño Sauce, 60
    Goat Cheese Basil Grits, 179
Grove Park Inn, 104
Guastavino, Rafael, 98

H

ham
    Creamy Red-Eye Gravy, 12
    Grilled Club Sandwich with Brie and
        Raspberry Honey Mayonnaise, 71
    Southern Chicken Saltimbocca with
        Country Ham in a Mushroom Marsala
        Sauce, 130–31
Henry, O., 98
Herb-Roasted Whole Chicken with Savory
    Pan Gravy, 136–37
Hickory Nut Gap Farm, 151
Highland Brewing, xv
honey, xv, 76, 213
Hunt, Richard Morris, 107

J

jalapeño
    Basic Barbecue Sauce, 21
    Chicken Andouille Stir-Fry with Orange
        Jalapeño Glaze, 134

Green Tomato Salsa, 7
Pickled Green Tomato Salad with Fresh
    Mozzarella, 86
Smoked Jalapeño Aiolo, 35
Smoked Jalapeño Sauce, 23
Sunshot Salsa, 8
Tupelo Honey Wing Sauce, 22

L

Lake Eden Arts Festival, 73
lamb
    Lamb and Multi-Mushroom Meat Loaf
        with Mint Glaze, 150
    Lamb and Root Vegetable Stew Topped
        with Grits Croutons, 162–63
    Parsley Crusted Lamb Chops with Dijon
        Demi-Glace, 147
Lamb and Multi-Mushroom Meat Loaf with
    Mint Glaze, 150
Lamb and Root Vegetable Stew Topped with
    Grits Croutons, 162–63
lardhouse, 2
LEAF festival, 181
Lee, Matt, 32
Lee, Ted, 32
Lemon Beurre Blanc, 117
Lemon Hollandaise, 106
Lemon Hollandaise Sauce, 106
Lemon Vinaigrette, 48
Look Homeward Angel (Wolfe, T.), 47
Looking Glass, 179
Low Country Gravy, 17

M

Macaroni and Gouda Casserole, 170–71
Maple Sweet Potato Pudding, 209
maple syrup
    Coconut Sweet Potato Bisque, 66
    Creamy Maple Mustard Dressing, 32
    Granola, 193
    Maple Sweet Potato Pudding, 209
    Pork and Blueberry Sausage Simmered in
        Maple Syrup, 153
    Smashed Sweet Potatoes, 128
Marinated Green Tomatoes, 111
marsala wine, 130–31, 157, 158
meat and three tradition, 166
meatloaf
    Chicken Apple Meat Loaf with Tarragon
        Tomato Gravy, 132–33
    Lamb and Multi-Mushroom Meat Loaf
        with Mint Glaze, 150
Memphis Minnie, 2
microbreweries, xv
Milk Gravy, 10
mint, fresh, Lamb and Multi-Mushroom
    Meat Loaf with Mint Glaze, 150
The Mixing Bowl local produce guide, 129
Mocha Cheesecake, 205
Mondo Mushroom Ragout, 172
Moog, Bob, xiv, 98

Morrison, Van, 44
Mount Mitchell, 15
Mountain Dance and Folk Festival, 181
Mountain Tailgate Market Association, 160
Mushroom Quesadilla with Green Tomato
    Salsa and Smoked Jalapeño Sauce,
    56–57
mushrooms
    Candied-Ginger Cornbread Dressing, 182
    Cremini Sweet Onion Gravy, 13
    Fried Green Tomato and Grilled
        Portobello Sandwich with Basil
        Roasted Red Pepper Mayonnaise, 79
    Lamb and Multi-Mushroom Meat Loaf
        with Mint Glaze, 150
    Mondo Mushroom Ragout, 172
    Mushroom Quesadilla with Green Tomato
        Salsa and Smoked Jalapeño Sauce,
        56–57
    Shiitake Sweet Potato Hash, 201
    Southern Chicken Saltimbocca with
        Country Ham in a Mushroom Marsala
        Sauce, 130–31
    Southern Spring Salad with Basil
        Vinaigrette, 91
music, xvii, 70, 98, 181

N

Neal, Bill, 101, 133, 145
New Orleans, xi
North Carolina Arboretum, 186, 197
Nut-Crusted Brie with Cabernet Balsamic–
    Glazed Figs, 52
nuts
    Almond-Crusted Trout with Blackened
        Crawfish and Roasted Red Pepper
        Butter, 112–13
    Basil Cashew Pesto, 33
    Blueberry Granola Crunch Pancakes, 192
    Chocolate Pecan Pie, 207
    Nut-Crusted Brie with Cabernet
        Balsamic–Glazed Figs, 52
    Nutty Fried Chicken with Smashed Sweet
        Potatoes and Milk Gravy, 127
    Pain Perdu with Cinnamon Sugar,
        Blueberry Preserves, and Toasted
        Almonds, 187
    Peach Cobbler with Candied Almonds,
        215
    Pecan Vinaigrette, 31
    Pecan-Crusted Red Snapper with Spiced
        Black Beans and Orange Cilantro
        Butter, 114
    Southern Spring Salad with Basil
        Vinaigrette, 91
    Spiced Pecans, 120
    Sweet Potato Pancakes with Peach
        Butter and Spiced Pecans, 199–200
Nutty Fried Chicken with Smashed Sweet
    Potatoes and Milk Gravy, 127

O

oats, Granola, 193
"Old Kentucky Home" boardinghouse, 47
Olmstead, Frederick Law, 98, 107
Olson, Charles, 70
Orange Cilantro Butter, 114, 115
Orange Cilantro Gravy, 19
orange marmalade
    Cherry Apple ZZ, 39
    Smoked Jalapeño Sauce, 23
    Tupelo Honey Wing Sauce, 22
oranges
    Chicken Andouille Stir-Fry with Orange
        Jalapeño Glaze, 134
    Orange Cilantro Butter, 114, 115
    Orange Cilantro Gravy, 19
    Smoked Jalapeño Sauce, 23
    Tupelo Honey Wings, 58
oregano, fresh, 56–57, 172
Oven-Roasted Tomatoes, 47

P

Pach Square, 102
Pack, George, xiv
Pain Perdu with Cinnamon Sugar, Blueberry
    Preserves, and Toasted Almonds, 187
pancakes
    Blueberry Granola Crunch Pancakes, 192
    Sweet Potato Pancakes with Peach
        Butter and Spiced Pecans, 199–200
Pan-Fried Pork Chops with Black-Eyed Pea
    and Andouille Sausage Ragout, 157
pantry, 2
Papazian, Charlie, xv
parsley, fresh, 29, 55, 147, 182, 190
Parsley Crusted Lamb Chops with Dijon
    Demi-Glace, 147
parsnip, 162–63, 174
Peach Butter, 40
Peach Cobbler with Candied Almonds, 215
Peach Fennel Salsa, 5
peaches
    Char-Grilled Pork Tenderloin with Peach
        Fennel Salsa, 155
    Peach Butter, 40
    Peach Cobbler with Candied Almonds, 215
    Peach Fennel Salsa, 5
    Peachy Grilled Chicken Salad with Pecan
        Vinaigrette, 89
Peachy Grilled Chicken Salad with Pecan
    Vinaigrette, 89
peanut butter, Fit for the King Peanut
    Butter and Banana Sandwich, 73
Pecan Vinaigrette, 31
Pecan-Crusted Red Snapper with Spiced
    Black Beans and Orange Cilantro
    Butter, 114
pecans
    Chocolate Pecan Pie, 207
    Pecan Vinaigrette, 31
    Pecan-Crusted Red Snapper with Spiced

Black Beans and Orange Cilantro
        Butter, 114
    Spiced Pecans, 200
    Sweet Potato Pancakes with Peach
        Butter and Spiced Pecans, 199–200
Perkinson, Annie Louise, 151
Perkinson, Isaiah, 151
Pickled Onion Aioli, 121
Pickled Sweet Onions, 41
pie dough, 138–39, 141
    Broccoli and New Potato Quiche, 196
    Chocolate Pecan Pie, 207
    Tomato Pie, 190
Pisgah Brewing, xv
poblano pepper
    Apple Salsa, 4
    Blackened Chicken Potpie, 138–39
    Chicken Apple Meat Loaf with Tarragon
        Tomato Gravy, 132–33
    Grateful Dead Black Bean Burger with
        Cilantro Lime Mayonnaise, 81
    Salsa Verde Pinto Beans, 180
pork
    Andouille Sausage Ragout, 158
    Buttermilk Pork Chops with Creamy Red-
        Eye Gravy, 146
    Char-Grilled Pork Tenderloin with Peach
        Fennel Salsa, 155
    Chicken Andouille Stir-Fry with Orange
        Jalapeño Glaze, 134
    Chorizo-Baked Sea Scallops with Basil
        Cream Sauce, 103
    Pan-Fried Pork Chops with Black-Eyed Pea
        and Andouille Sausage Ragout, 157
    Pork and Blueberry Sausage Simmered in
        Maple Syrup, 153
    Root Beer Molasses–Glazed Pork
        Tenderloin with Smoked Jalapeño
        Sauce and Apple Salsa, 149
    Sausage Gravy, 10
Pork and Blueberry Sausage Simmered in
    Maple Syrup, 153
Portobello mushrooms, 79
potatoes
    Blackened Chicken Potpie, 138–39
    Broccoli and New Potato Quiche, 196
    Corn and Crab Chowder, 67
    Lamb and Root Vegetable Stew Topped
        with Grits Croutons, 162–63
preserves and pickles, 36
    Blackberry Skillet Jam, 38
    Blueberry Preserves, 37
    Cherry Apple Chowchow, 39
    Peach Butter, 40
    Pickled Sweet Onions, 41
pudding
    Banana Pudding, 208
    Griddled Blackberry Breakfast Bread
        Pudding, 195
    Maple Sweet Potato Pudding, 209

R

raspberries
    Raspberry Honey Mayonnaise, 34
    Three-Berry Cream Cheese Pie, 212
Rauschenberg, Robert, 70
Reuben with Chowchow, Swiss Cheese, and
    Thousand Island Dijonnaise, 74
"Rhapsody in Blue," 98
Roasted Corn Salsa, 6
roasted garlic oil, 5
roasted garlic puree, 5
Romaine lettuce, 71, 83
root beer
    Basic Barbecue Sauce, 21
    Root Beer Molasses–Glazed Pork
        Tenderloin with Smoked Jalapeño
        Sauce and Apple Salsa, 149
    Root Beer–Sorghum Molasses Glaze, 24
Root Beer Molasses–Glazed Pork Tenderloin
    with Smoked Jalapeño Sauce and
    Apple Salsa, 149
Root Beer–Sorghum Molasses Glaze, 24
rosemary, fresh, 111, 136–37, 155, 158,
    162–63, 172
Rosemary Aioli, 111
Roux, 17
rutabaga, 162–63

S

sage, fresh, 6, 17, 18, 56–57, 130–31,
    136–37, 158, 162–63, 172, 182, 201
salads, 70
    Bacony Egg Salad, 87
    Get Your Leafy Greens Quota Salad with
        Sherry Vinaigrette, 94
    Peachy Grilled Chicken Salad with Pecan
        Vinaigrette, 89
    Pickled Green Tomato Salad with Fresh
        Mozzarella, 86
    Southern Spring Salad with Basil
        Vinaigrette, 91
    Spinach Salad with Roasted Beets, Goat
        Cheese, Peppered Bacon, and Garlic
        Ranch Dressing, 90
    Tupelo Honey Coleslaw, 93
salsa, 3
    Apple Salsa, 4
    Green Tomato Salsa, 7
    Peach Fennel Salsa, 5
    Roasted Corn Salsa, 6
    Salsa Verde Pinto Beans, 180
    Sunshot Salsa, 8
Salsa Verde Pinto Beans, 180
sandwiches, 70
    Fit for the King Peanut Butter and
        Banana Sandwich, 73
    Fried Green Tomato and Grilled
        Portobello Sandwich with Basil
        Roasted Red Pepper Mayonnaise, 79
    Grateful Dead Black Bean Burger with
        Cilantro Lime Mayonnaise, 81

sandwiches (continued)
  Grilled Club Sandwich with Brie and Raspberry Honey Mayonnaise, 71
  Reuben with Chowchow, Swiss Cheese, and Thousand Island Dijonnaise, 74
  Southern Fried Chicken BLT, 83
  Tupelo Honey Chicken Sandwich with Havarti Cheese and Cranberry Mayonnaise, 76
sauces. See gravies and sauces
sausage
  Andouille Sausage Ragout, 158
  Chicken Andouille Stir-Fry with Orange Jalapeño Glaze, 134
  Chorizo-Baked Sea Scallops with Basil Cream Sauce, 103
  Pan-Fried Pork Chops with Black-Eyed Pea and Andouille Sausage Ragout, 157
  Pork and Blueberry Sausage Simmered in Maple Syrup, 153
  Sausage Gravy, 10
Sausage Gravy, 10
Savory Pan Gravy, 136–37
scallops, Chorizo-Baked Sea Scallops with Basil Cream Sauce, 103
seafood. See fish and seafood
Seared Crab Cakes and Lemon Hollandaise, 104–5
"Selling My Pork Chops," 2
Sherry Vinaigrette, 95
Shiitake Sweet Potato Hash, 201
side dishes. See the threes
Shoo-Mercy, 173
Shrimp and Goat Cheese Grits with Roasted Red Pepper Sauce, 101
Smashed Sweet Potatoes, 128
Smoked Jalapeño Aiolo, 35
Smoked Jalapeño Sauce, 9, 23, 56–57
Smoked Jalapeño–Glazed New York Strip Steak with Tomato Shallot Gravy, 159
Smoked Salmon–Wrapped Sea Scallops with Capers and Pickled Onion Aioli, 121
Smoked Tomato Sauce, 20
Smoked Tomatoes and Jalapeños, 28, 60
smokehouse, 2, 144
sorghum, 9
sorghum molasses, 21, 24, 149
soups, 44, 61
  Carolina Fish Chowder, 65
  Cheesy Onion Bisque, 63
  Coconut Sweet Potato Bisque, 66
  Corn and Crab Chowder, 67
  Creamy Tomato Soup, 62
Southern Chicken Saltimbocca with Country Ham in a Mushroom Marsala Sauce, 130–31

Southern Fried Chicken BLT, 83
Southern Fried Chicken Breasts with Cremini Sweet Onion Gravy, 125
Spice-Crusted Tuna with Seared Crab Cakes and Lemon Hollandaise, 104
Spiced Black Beans, 115
Spiced Pecans, 200
Spicy Smoked Tomato Vinaigrette, 28
spinach, 90, 119
Spinach Salad with Roasted Beets, Goat Cheese, Peppered Bacon, and Garlic Ranch Dressing, 90
Spinning Spider, 179
St. Lawrence Basilica, 98
Sunday dinner tradition, 166
Sunshot Farm, 15
Sunshot Organics, xiv
Sunshot Salsa, 8, 60
Sweet Potato Pancakes with Peach Butter and Spiced Pecans, 199–200
sweet potatoes, 66, 128, 199–200, 201, 209
Swiss chard, 94, 116–17

T
Tailgate Markets, 160
Tarragon Tomato Gravy, 133
THC Granola, 193
Thousand Island Dressing, 75
Three-Berry Cream Cheese Pie, 212
the threes
  Beets My Heart, 174
  Benne-Coated Asparagus, 167
  Candied-Ginger Cornbread Dressing, 182
  Cheesy Mashed Cauliflower, 175
  Fried Green Tomatoes with Goat Cheese Basil Grits, 178
  Macaroni and Gouda Casserole, 170–71
  Mondo Mushroom Ragout, 172
  Salsa Verde Pinto Beans, 180
  Tupelo Honey Pickled Beet Salad, 169
  Tupelo Honey–Glazed Carrots, 177
thyme, fresh, 18, 20, 56–57, 67, 136–37, 138–39, 158, 162–63, 172
tomatillos, 180
tomato, 19, 65, 71, 91, 94
  Creamy Tomato Soup, 62
  Curry-Spiced Halibut with Chard and Oven-Roasted Tomatoes in Lemon Beurre Blanc, 116–17
  Oven-Roasted Tomatoes, 47
  Smoked Tomato Sauce, 20
  Southern Fried Chicken BLT, 83
  Spicy Smoked Tomato Vinaigrette, 28
  Sunshot Salsa, 8
  Tarragon Tomato Gravy, 133

Tomato Pie, 190
  Tomato Shallot Gravy, 16
Tomato Pie, 190
Tomato Shallot Gravy, 16
Traditional Appalachian Chow Chow, 75
truffles, black, 18
tuna, Spice-Crusted Tuna with Seared Crab Cakes and Lemon Hollandaise, 104
tupelo honey, xv
  Apple Salsa, 4
  Chocolate Pecan Pie, 207
  Fit for the King Peanut Butter and Banana Sandwich, 73
  Pecan Vinaigrette, 31
  Raspberry Honey Mayonnaise, 34
  Shiitake Sweet Potato Hash, 201
  Smoked Jalapeño Sauce, 23
  Sweet Potato Pancakes with Peach Butter and Spiced Pecans, 199–200
  Tupelo Honey Pickled Beet Salad, 169
  Tupelo Honey Wing Sauce, 22
  Tupelo Honey Wings, 58
  Tupelo Honey–Glazed Carrots, 177
Tupelo Honey Cafe, xi, xiii–xv, 2, 9
Tupelo Honey Cafe Granola, 193
Tupelo Honey Chicken Marinade, 77
Tupelo Honey Chicken Sandwich with Havarti Cheese and Cranberry Mayonnaise, 76
Tupelo Honey Ginormous Biscuits, 189
Tupelo Honey Pickled Beet Salad, 169
Tupelo Honey Wing Sauce, 22
Tupelo Honey Wings, 58
Tupelo Honey–Glazed Carrots, 177
turkey
  Grilled Club Sandwich with Brie and Raspberry Honey Mayonnaise, 71
  Turkey Apple Meat Loaf with Tarragon Tomato Gravy, 132–33
turnips, 162–63, 174
Twain, Mark, 124
Twombly, Cy, 70

V
Vanderbilt, George, xiv, 44, 107

W
Warm Pimento Cheese and Chips, 55
Williams, William Carlos, 73
wine and beer pairings, xvii
Wolfe, Julia, 44, 50
Wolfe, Thomas, xiv, 44, 50, 98

Y
Yellow Branch Farm, 179
You Can't Go Home Again (Wolfe, T.), 47